The Wilderness
Directory

*A Quick-Reference Guide
to America's Wilderness*

Edited by Russ Schneider

THE WILDERNESS SOCIETY · FOUNDED IN 1935 ·

FALCON®

HELENA, MONTANA

©1998 Falcon® Publishing, Inc., Helena, Montana

Printed in Canada.

1 2 3 4 5 6 7 8 9 0 TP 03 02 01 00 99 98

Editing, design, typesetting, and other pre-press work by Falcon,®
Helena, Montana.

Cover photo by Eric Wunrow.

Library of Congress Cataloging-in-Publication Data:

The Wilderness Directory : a quick-reference guide to America's wilderness /
    produced in cooperation with The Wilderness Society and edited by
    Russ Schneider.
        p.   cm.
    Includes index.
    ISBN 1-56044-669-2 (pbk. : alk. paper)
    1. Wilderness areas—United States—Directories.   I. Schneider,
Russ. II. Wilderness Society.
QH76.W555 1998
333.78'2'02573—dc21
                                                    98-26496
                                                    CIP

Contents

Preface

The Wilderness Directory is a joint effort between The Wilderness Society and Falcon Publishing to provide wilderness visitors with a thorough, but compact and user-friendly book listing all the wilderness areas in the United States. These pages contain a complete and up-to-date list of America's 634 wilderness areas. Our goal—to create a convenient, usable list of contacts and information for the purpose and ease of planning your wilderness visits—was a challenge to reach, but we are thrilled with the results.

This project would not have been possible without the help of the National Park Service, United States Department of Agriculture Forest Service, U.S. Fish and Wildlife Service, and the Bureau of Land Management; they provided informative web pages and other information about our public lands. In addition, this project would not have been finished accurately without the help of Kurt Redenbo of The Wilderness Society, Erin Turner and Larissa Berry of Falcon Publishing, and the regional directors of The Wilderness Society.

Introduction

Something will have gone out of us as a people if we ever let the remaining wilderness be destroyed.

— Wallace Stegner, author, and
former Wilderness Society
Governing Council member

THE IMPORTANCE OF WILDERNESS

Wilderness is a place for solitude and inspiration—a place to get away from it all. At the same time, designated wilderness protects biodiversity, the web of life.

Of 261 basic ecosystem types in the United States, 157 are represented in the wilderness system. Without these large, ecologically complex areas of preserved landscape, species protection would be virtually impossible, and our continuing understanding of natural systems would be reduced to speculation. Designated wilderness protects ecology, which is vital to all of us:

- Wilderness areas protect watersheds that provide drinking water to many cities and rural communities.

- Wilderness serves as critical habitat for wildlife threatened by extinction.

- Wilderness helps filter and improve the quality of our air.

- Wilderness maintains gene pools that help to protect biodiversity and provide a natural "laboratory" for research.

- Wilderness helps meet the nation's increasing demand for outdoor recreation: hiking, hunting, fishing, bird watching, canoeing, camping, and many other activities.

- Wilderness is a haven, providing places away from the pressures of our fast-paced, industrialized society where we can seek relief from the noise, haste, and crowds that too often confine us.

HOW IS WILDERNESS DESIGNATED?

The Wilderness Act of 1964 directed the Forest Service, National Park Service, and the U.S. Fish and Wildlife Service to survey their roadless lands for possible wilderness designation. The act requires that wilderness areas be "administered for the use and enjoyment of the American people in such a manner as will leave them unimpaired for future use and enjoyment as wilderness."

The Wilderness Act protects designated wilderness areas from roads, dams, or other permanent structures; from timber cutting and the operation of motorized vehicles and equipment; and, since 1984, from new mining claims and mineral leasing.

Two other laws require reviews of potential wilderness on national land. The Federal Land Policy and Management

Act of 1976 (FLPMA) directed the Bureau of Land Management to take inventory of its roadless land for wilderness protection; and the Alaska Lands Act of 1980 also called for reviews.

Each federal land-management agency can recommend to Congress, on a state-by-state basis, land that qualifies for wilderness designation. Congress then decides which areas to designate. In many cases, Congress has designated more land for wilderness than an agency recommended.

Mining operations and livestock grazing are permitted in wilderness areas where such operations existed before the area became designated wilderness. Hunting and fishing are also allowed in designated wilderness areas (with the exception of hunting in national parks) as are a wide range of other non-mechanized recreational, scientific, and outdoor activities.

The Wilderness Society

THE WILDERNESS SOCIETY'S ROOTS

When their car came to a screeching halt somewhere outside of Knoxville, Tennessee, the four passengers were in hot debate over plans for a new conservation group. The men got out of the car and climbed an embankment where they sat and argued over the philosophy and definition of the new organization.

Three months later, in January 1935, the group met again in Washington, D.C. Participants in the meeting included Robert Sterling Yard, publicist for the National Park Service; Benton MacKaye, the "Father of the Appalachian Trail"; and Robert Marshall, chief of recreation and lands for the USDA Forest Service. "All we desire to save from invasion," they declared, "is that extremely minor fraction of outdoor America which yet remains free from mechanical sights and sounds and smell." For a name, they finally settled on The Wilderness Society.

Among the cofounders was Aldo Leopold, a wildlife ecologist at the University of Wisconsin. In Leopold's view, The Wilderness Society would help form the cornerstone of a movement needed to save America's vanishing wilderness.

It took nearly thirty years, but President Lyndon B. Johnson finally signed The Wilderness Act of 1964 into law September 3rd, in the rose garden of the White House.

THE WILDERNESS SOCIETY TODAY

The founders called their organization The Wilderness Society, and they put out an urgent call, as we do today, for "spirited people who will fight for the freedom of the wilderness."

Today, Americans enjoy some 104 million acres of protected wilderness, due in large part to the efforts of The Wilderness Society. The Wilderness Society is a nonprofit organization devoted to creating a nationwide network of wildlands and fostering an American land ethic. You can help protect American wildlands by becoming a Wilderness Society Member. Here are three ways you can join:

- Telephone: 1-800-THE-WILD
- E-mail: member@tws.org or visit the website: www.wilderness.org
- Write: The Wilderness Society, Attention: Membership, 900 17th St. Northwest, Washington, D.C. 20006

Using this Directory

Wilderness areas listed in this book were designated by the Wilderness Act of 1964 or by Congress before 1998 and managed by regional agencies as units of the National Wilderness Preservation System. All wilderness areas are listed alphabetically under each state. If a wilderness area includes acreage in two or more states, the entry for that wilderness area will appear only in the state with the largest amount of acreage. A cross-reference entry will appear in all other states with wilderness acreage of the same name. Each entry includes:

Official name of the wilderness area: The name as listed in the federal database. If a wilderness area is commonly known by another name or commonly grouped with another wilderness area, this information will be noted in the description.

Managing agency: Bureau of Land Management, USDA Forest Service, U.S. Fish and Wildlife Service, or National Park Service.

Phone number of managing agency: This number is usually the manager's office closest to the wilderness area, but in some cases may be an umbrella agency's number under whose jurisdiction the wilderness area falls. In several states, this number may take you to the regional public information center for national forests or wilderness areas.

Year Established: "Est." and the year indicates the year Congress passed legislation to officially designate each area.

This date may or may not correspond to the founding of a park or monument. Wilderness designation is specific and independent from other designations. In cases where wilderness was designated in one year but acreage was added later, only the first year of designation appears.

Abbreviations	
BLM	Wilderness area managed by the Bureau of Land Management.
NF	National forest managed by the USDA Forest Service.
NWR	National Wildlife Refuge managed by the U.S. Fish and Wildlife Service.
NP	National Park managed by the National Park Service.
NM	National Monument managed by the National Park Service.
NS	National Seashore managed by the National Park Service.
NR	National River managed by the National Park Service.
NCA	National Conservation Area managed by the Bureau of Land Management.
NRA	National Recreation Area, often managed cooperatively by several agencies or the USDA Forest Service.

Acres

- •For wilderness areas in our national forests, the acreage total came from the USDA Forest Service federal database: http://www.fs.fed.us/database/lar/lartab7.htm This is the "Total Acreage" column from Table 7—National Wilderness Areas by State for USDAFS Wilderness Areas.

- •For wilderness areas in national parks, the acreage total came from the website http://www.nps.gov/partner/nwpsnps.html, Table: Wilderness in the NPS: Through the Years as published in the Federal Register.

- •For wilderness areas in national wildlife refuges, the acreage total came from the website http://www.fws.gov/~r9realty/table10.html, Table: Wilderness Areas in National Wildlife Refuges and Fish Hatcheries.

- •For wilderness area in Bureau of Land Management units, the acreage total came from other BLM sources.

Geophysical reference: A statement about topography or the geophysical reference and ecosystem type follows information about acreage. Ecosystem types include desert, alpine, tundra, grassland, dry forest, mountain forest, temperate rainforest, deciduous forest, temperate evergreen forest, tropical rainforest, wetland, and so on. Geophysical references include mountain, plain, plateau, island, rolling hills, and so on.

What to see: Next, after the geophysical reference, each entry includes a unique natural feature, habitat, species, or designation within the area, including Wild and Scenic Rivers, National Scenic Trails, and other special designations.

Abbreviations	
W & SR	Wild and Scenic River
PCT	Pacific Crest Trail
AT	Appalachian Trail
CDT	Continental Divide Trail
NCT	North Country Trail

Location: A nearby town is listed for geographic reference, usually the nearest town or city with 10,000 people or more, but in some cases the town listed may have a smaller population. In Alaska, "near" may be a stretch. The closest town may not be very close to the area, but still the one closest.

Access and recreation symbols: Access methods, popular recreational opportunities, and fees or permits required are listed here. Because not all sites are accessible or contain recreational opportunities, this information is not included with all entries.

Symbols	
	HIKING
	BOAT OR PLANE ACCESS ONLY*
	PADDLING OR CANOEING
	FISHING
	ROCK CLIMBING OR MOUNTAINEERING
$	FEES, PERMITS, AND/OR GROUP SIZE LIMITATIONS
*Floatplane access on Alaska sites only.	

State-by-State Listing of Wilderness Areas

ALABAMA

Cheaha Talladega NF, 256-362-2909. Est. 1983.
  7,245 acres: deciduous mountain forest.
  Tremendous views atop quartz-streaked rock outcrops.
  Near Anniston.

Sipsey William Bankhead NF, 205-489-5112. Est. 1975.
  25,002 acres: deciduous mountain forest.
  Many waterfalls and the Sipsey Fork West W & SR.
  Near Decatur. $

ALASKA

Admiralty Island (*see* Kootznoowoo).

Aleutian Islands Alaska Maritime NWR, 907-235-6546. Est. 1980.
  1.3 million acres: remote islands.
  Crucial habitat for the stellar sea lions and many marine birds.
  Near Unalaska.

Andreafsky Yukon Delta NWR, 907-543-3151. Est. 1980.
  1.3 million acres: riparian and mountain tundra.
  Brown bears, wolves, salmon, and the Andreafsky River W & SR.
  Near Bethel.

Arctic Arctic NWR, 907-456-0250. Est. 1980.
  8 million acres: tundra and shrubland.
  Crucial wintering habitat for the Porcupine Caribou Herd.
  Near Fairbanks.

Becharof Becharof NWR, 907-246-3339. Est. 1980.
  400,000 acres: lakeside tundra wetlands.
  Brown bear, caribou, moose, and scenic Becharof Lake.
  Near Kodiak.

Bering Sea Alaska Maritime NWR, 907-235-6546. Est. 1970.
  81,340 acres: island tundra.
  These remote areas offer nesting habitat for McKay's bunting and
    scenic St. Matthews Island.
  Near Unalaska.

Bogoslof Alaska Maritime NWR, 907-235-6546. Est. 1970.
  175 acres: remote islands.
  Frequent volcanic events.
  Near Unalaska.

Chamisso Alaska Maritime NWR, 907-235-6546. Est. 1975.
  455 acres: remote islands.
  Best known for Puffin Island and its population of horned puffins.
  Near Unalaska.

Chuck River Tongass NF, 907-772-5934. Est. 1990.
  74,990 acres: temperate coastal forest.
  Often grouped with the Duncan Salt and Petersberg Creek
    Wilderness Areas; features healthy king salmon runs.
  Near Petersburg.

Coronation Island Tongass NF, 907-772-5934. Est. 1980.
  19,232 acres: temperate coastal forest.
  Sea otters, wolves, and black-tailed deer; rugged coastline.
  Near Craig.

Denali Denali NP, 907-683-2294. Est. 1980.
  2.124 million acres: tundra and alpine park.
  North America's highest point, 20,320-foot Mount McKinley
    (Denali) is found in this area.
  Near Anchorage. 🐾 🐚 ◊ $

Endicott River Tongass NF, 907-772-5934. Est. 1980.
  98,729 acres: temperate forest and alpine tundra.
  Brown bears and eagles; salmon run up the Endicott River.
  Near Juneau. 🚁 ✓ 🐚 🐾

Forrester Island Alaska Maritime NWR, 907-235-6546. Est. 1970.
  2,832 acres: temperate mountain forest.
  Prolific populations of exotic sea birds.
  Near Unalaska. 🚁

Gates of the Arctic Gates of the Arctic NP, 907-456-0281. Est. 1980.
  7.167 million acres: tundra and boreal forest.
  Vast and almost no evidence of human activity. Dall sheep and brown
    bears are common.
  Near Fairbanks. 🐚 🐾

Glacier Bay Glacier Bay NP, 907-697-2230. Est. 1980.
  2.77 million acres: glacial bay and temperate rainforest.
  Whales and calving glaciers.
  Near Juneau. 🐚 🐾

Hazy Islands Alaska Maritime NWR, 907-235-6546. Est. 1970.
  32 acres: remote islands.
  Rare sea birds.
  Near Unalaska. 🚁

Innoko Innoko NWR, 907-524-3251. Est. 1980.
  1.24 million acres: wetland and tundra.
  The wild Iditarod (of sled dog fame), Innoko, and Yetna rivers.
  Near McGrath. ✓ 🐾

Izembek Izembek NWR, 907-532-2445. Est. 1980.
   300,000 acres: lagoons and tundra.
   The world's largest eelgrass bed.
   Near Unalaska.

Karta Tongass NF, 907-772-5934. Est. 1990.
   39,894 acres: temperate coastal forest.
   Black bears, black-tailed deer, and the Karta River.
   Near Craig.

Katmai Katmai NP, 907-246-3305. Est. 1980.
   3.348 million acres: forest, wetland, and alpine park.
   Well known for photographs of brown bears feeding on salmon in
      Brooks River Falls.
   Near Anchorage.

Kenai Kenai NWR, 907-262-7021. Est. 1980.
   1.35 million acres: temperate mountain forest and lowlands.
   Healthy population of moose on the Kenai Peninsula and in the Kenai
      Mountains.
   Near Soldatna.

Kobuk Valley Western Arctic NP, 907-442-8300. Est. 1980.
   174,545 acres: mountains and tundra.
   This tundra valley ecosystem surrounds the Kobuk W & SR.
   Near Kotzebue.

Kootznoowoo Tongass NF, 907-772-5934. Est. 1980.
   74,990 acres: coastal temperate forest.
   Better known as Admiralty Island, 90 percent of Admiralty Island
      NM is designated Kootznoowoo Wilderness. Best known for
      heavy concentrations of brown bears.
   Near Juneau.

Koyukuk Koyukuk NWR, 907-656-1231. Est. 1980.
> 400,000 acres: wetland, tundra, and forest.
> The Nowitna W & SR supports abundant waterfowl and wild salmon.
> Near Kotzebue.

Kuiu Tongass NF, 907-772-5934. Est. 1990.
> 60,581 acres: temperate coastal forest.
> Often grouped with Tebenkof Bay Wilderness. Kuiu Island supports
>   sea lions, bears, and wolves.
> Near Petersburg.

Lake Clark Lake Clark NP, 907-271-3751. Est. 1980.
> 2.619 million acres: tundra, mountains, glaciers, and bays.
> Bristol Bay is one of the world's largest sockeye salmon and crab
>   fishing grounds.
> Near Anchorage.

Maurelle Islands Tongass NF, 907-772-5934. Est. 1980.
> 4,937 acres: temperate coastal forest.
> Often grouped with nearby Coronation Island and Warren Island,
>   featuring rugged coastlines, sea otters, bears, wolves, and black-
>   tailed deer.
> Near Ketchikan.

Misty Fiords Misty Fiords NM, 907-225-2148. Est. 1980.
> 2.142 million acres: temperate coastal forest.
> Better known as Misty Fiords National Monument. Features
>   abundant wildlife, blue-green waters, and pleasant cruising by
>   boat.
> Near Ketchikan.

Noatak Western Arctic NP, 907-442-8300. Est. 1980.
> 5.76 million acres: mountains and tundra.
> Features the Noatak W & SR.
> Near Kotzebue.

Nunivak Yukon Delta NWR, 907-543-3151. Est. 1980.
600,00 acres: island and tundra.
Introduced reindeer, steep shoreline cliffs, and sea birds.
Near Bethel.

Petersburg Creek–Duncan Creek Tongass NF, 907-772-5934. Est. 1980.
46,849 acres: temperate mountain forest.
Often grouped with Salt Creek and Chuck River; area supports sea
otters, bears, wolves, and black-tailed deer.
Near Petersburg. ⌒⁄

Pleasant-Lemusurier-Inian Tongass NF, 907-772-5934. Est. 1990.
23,151 acres: temperate coastal forest.
Rugged straits and cliff-dwelling sea birds.
Near Glacier Bay National Park and Hoonah. ✈

Russell Fiord Tongass NF, 907-772-5934. Est. 1980.
348,701 acres: glaciers and temperate coastal forest.
Incredible glacier viewing and frequent whale sightings.
Near Sitka. ✈ 🐾 🛶 ⌒

Saint Lazaria Alaska Maritime NWR, 907-235-6546. Est. 1970.
65 acres: volcanic island.
Rare sea birds and harsh barren rock habitat.
Near Unalaska. ✈

Selawik Selawik NWR, 907-442-3799. Est. 1980.
240,000 acres: tundra wetlands.
Possible location of Bering Land Bridge and important sheefish
habitat.
Near Kotzebue.

Semidi Alaska Maritime NWR, 907-235-6546. Est. 1980.
  250,000 acres: islands and tundra.
  Nesting horned puffins and Aleutian Canada geese.
  Near Unalaska.

Simeonof Alaska Maritime NWR, 907-235-6546. Est. 1980.
  250,000 acres: islands and tundra.
  Surrounding waters support productive crab populations.
  Near Unalaska.

South Baranof Tongass NF, 907-772-5934. Est. 1980.
  319,568 acres: temperate coastal forest.
  Deep valleys, glaciers, hidden inlets for whale watching.
  Near Sitka.

South Etolin Islands Tongass NF, 907-772-5934. Est. 1990.
  83,371 acres: temperate mountain forest.
  Forested valleys, inlets, alpine meadows, and glaciers provide habitat
    for elk, black bears, salmon, and whales.
  Near Ketchikan.

South Prince of Wales Tongass NF, 907-772-5934. Est. 1980.
  91,018 acres: temperate coastal forest.
  Southern Prince of Wales Island, covered with hemlock and spruce,
    supports wolves, black bears, and black-tailed deer.
  Near Petersburg.

Stikine-Leconte Tongass NF, 907-772-5934. Est. 1980.
  449,951 acres: temperate coastal forest.
  The Stikine River and rugged coastlines support abundant wildlife.
    Salmon runs draw one of the largest concentrations of bald eagles
    in the U.S.
  Near Petersburg.

Tebenkof Bay Tongass NF, 907-772-5934. Est. 1980.
   66,839 acres: temperate coastal forest.
   Often grouped with Kuiu, an intricate network of inlets and bays
      makes this a popular area for sea kayakers.
   Near Petersburg.

Togiak Togiak NWR, 907-842-1063. Est. 1980.
   2.27 million acres: coastal tundra and wetland.
   Its many rivers are famous for salmon fishing.
   Near Dillingham.

Tracy Arm–Fords Terror Tongass NF, 907-772-5934. Est. 1980.
   653,179 acres: temperate coastal forest.
   Rough and wild glacial carved valleys and ice-choked fjords provide
      habitat for killer whales, bald eagles, and other wildlife.
   Near Sitka.

Tuxedni Alaska Maritime NWR, 907-235-6546. Est. 1970.
   5,566 acres: remote islands.
   Surrounding waters support productive sea life.
   Near Unalaska.

Unimak Izembek NWR, 907-532-2445. Est. 1980.
   910,000 acres: island wetlands and ice fields.
   Unimak Island, brown bears, and good salmon runs.
   Near Unalaska.

Warren Island Tongass NF, 907-772-5934. Est. 1980.
   11,181 acres: temperate coastal forest.
   Often grouped with Maurelle and Coronation Island; heavy rains
      and temperate rainforest.
   Near Ketchikan.

West Chichagof–Yakobi Tongass NF, 907-772-5934. Est. 1980.
  265,529 acres: temperate coastal forest.
  Yakobi and Chichagof Islands have many rocky inlets, tidal plains,
    and grasslands.
  Near Sitka.

Wrangell–Saint Elias Wrangell–Saint Elias NP, 907-822-5234. Est. 1980.
  8.7 million acres: alpine and temperate forest.
  Nation's largest wilderness area and the largest assemblage of glaciers
    and peaks over 16,000 feet in North America.
  Near Valdez.

ARIZONA

Apache Creek Prescott NF, 520-771-4700. Est. 1984.
  5,666 acres: arid forest and rolling hills.
  Dry pine forest supports healthy populations of deer and mountain
    lions.
  Near Prescott.

Aravaipa Canyon Safford BLM, 520-348-4400. Est. 1984.
  19,410 acres: arid canyon and tablelands.
  Aravaipa Creek Canyon is a popular float and adventure area.
  Near Safford. $

Arrastra Mountains Kingman BLM, 520-692-4400. Est. 1990.
  129,800 acres: desert mountains and canyon pools.
  In Peoples Canyon there is a 2-mile-long chain of deep connected
    pools.
  Near Kingman.

Aubrey Peak Kingman BLM, 520-692-4400. Est. 1990
  15,400 acres: desert mesas and buttes.
  Mix of vegetation in the Mohave/Sonoran Desert transition zone.
  Near Kingman.

Babaquivari Tuscon BLM, 520-722-4289. Est. 1990.
    2,065 acres: desert and arid mountain forest.
    7,730-foot Babaquivari Peak dominates the skyline.
    Near Sells.

Bear Wallow Apache-Sitgreaves NF, 520-333-4301. Est. 1984.
    11,080 acres: arid mountain forest.
    Bear Wallow Creek supports the rare Apache trout.
    Near Springerville.

Beaver Dam Mountains Arizona Strip BLM, 435-688-3200. Est. 1984.
    19,600 acres (2,597 in Utah): mountain desert and shrubland.
    The Virgin River is popular for paddlers and crucial habitat for the
        endangered woodfin minnow.
    Near St. George, Utah.

Big Horn Mountains Phoenix BLM, 602-580-5500. Est. 1990.
    21,000 acres: mountains and desert plain.
    Mountains support desert bighorn sheep, Gila monsters, and the
        desert tortoise.
    Near Phoenix.

Cabeza Prieta Cabreza Prieta NWR, 520-387-6483. Est. 1990.
    803,418 acres: mountains and desert.
    Granite peaks and valleys dotted with sand dunes and lava flows
        provide habitat for the Sonoran Desert pronghorn.
    Near Ajo.

Castle Creek Prescott NF, 520-771-4700. Est. 1984.
    25,215 acres: desert and arid forest.
    Intact stands of old-growth ponderosa pine and alligator juniper.
    Near Prescott.

Cedar Bench Prescott NF, 520-771-4700. Est. 1984.
14,950 acres: desert and arid forest.
The Verde W & SR forms a portion of its eastern boundary and is essential riparian habitat.
Near Prescott. 🥾

Note: There are two separate Chiricahua Wilderness Areas managed by different agencies.

Chiricahua Coronado NF, 520-670-4552. Est. 1964.
87,700 acres: desert and arid forest.
Once home of Chiricahua and Cochise Apaches, still the "Wonder land of Rocks."
Near Willcox. 🥾 🐾

Chiricahua Chiricahua NM, 520-824-3560. Est. 1976.
9,440 acres: desert and volcanic spires.
Once home of Chiricahua and Cochise Apaches, it is still the "Wonderland of Rocks."
Near Willcox. 🥾 🐾 $

Cottonwood Point Arizona Strip BLM, 435-688-3200. Est. 1984.
6,860 acres: cliffs, canyons, and arid forest.
Features multicolored sandstone cliffs and craggy pinnacles.
Near Colorado City. 🥾

Coyote Mountains Tuscon BLM, 520-722-4289. Est. 1990.
5,080 acres: mountains, desert, and arid forest.
Features rugged peaks in the Coyote Mountains. Habitat for small desert mammals and their predators.
Near Tucson. 🥾 🐾

Dos Cabezas Safford BLM, 520-348-4400. Est. 1990.
11,700 acres: mountain desert and shrubland.
The upper portions of Buckeye Canyon harbor the unique collared lizard.
Near Safford. 🥾

Eagletail Yuma BLM, 520-317-3200. Est. 1990.
  100,600 acres: desert mountains and plains.
  Fifteen miles of the Eagletail Mountains with natural arches, spires, and monoliths.
  Near Yuma.

East Cactus Plain Lake Havasu BLM, 520-505-1200. Est. 1990.
  14,630 acres: desert and dunes.
  Known for the unique "dunescrub" vegetation.
  Near Parker.

Escudilla Apache NF, 520-339-4384. Est. 1984.
  5,200 acres: desert mountains and arid forest.
  Features 10,912-foot Escudilla Mountain.
  Near Alpine.

Fishhooks Safford BLM, 520-348-4400. Est. 1990.
  10,500 acres: desert canyons and arid forest.
  Features 6,693-foot Gila Peak.
  Near Safford.

Fossil Springs Coconino NF, 520-527-3660. Est. 1984.
  22,149 acres: desert canyon.
  Fossil Springs supports an abundance of desert wildlife.
  Near Camp Verde.

Four Peaks Tonto NF, 602-225-5200. Est. 1984.
  61,074 acres: arid mountain forest.
  Abundant wildlife including black bears, desert bighorn sheep, and ring-tailed cats.
  Near Mesa.

Galiuro Coronado NF, 520-670-4552. Est. 1964.
   76,317 acress: arid forest and desert canyons.
   Diverse forest of Arizona cypress and sycamore to Mexican white pine.
   Near Tucson. 🥾

Gibraltar Mountain Lake Havasu BLM, 520-505-1200. Est. 1990.
   17,790 acres: desert canyons and mountains.
   The eroded volcanic tuff beds have many alcoves and caves.
   Near Lake Havasu City. 🥾 ⛓

Grand Wash Cliffs Arizona Strip BLM, 435-688-3200. Est. 1984.
   37,030 acres: desert, shrubland, and arid forest.
   Important habitat for the desert tortoise, Gila monster, and desert
      bighorn sheep.
   Near St. George, Utah. 🥾 ⛓

Granite Mountain Prescott NF, 520-771-4700. Est. 1984.
   9,762 acres: arid mountain forest.
   Uniquely shaped alligator juniper and ancient yellow-bark pine.
   Near Prescott. 🥾

Harcuvar Mountains Lake Havasu BLM, 520-505-1200. Est. 1990.
   25,050 acres: desert mountains.
   Isolated area with abundant wildlife.
   Near Lake Havasu City. 🥾 ⛓

Harquahala Phoenix BLM, 602-580-5500. Est. 1990.
   22,880 acres: desert mountains.
   5,691-foot Harquahala Peak, the highest point in southwest Arizona.
   Near Phoenix. 🥾

Hassayampa River Canyon Phoenix BLM, 602-580-5500. Est. 1990.
   11,840 acres: desert canyon.
   Features the free-flowing Hassayampa River and associated riparian
      habitat.
   Near Phoenix. 🥾 ⛓

Havasu Havasu NWR, 760-326-3853. Est. 1990.
> 17,606 acres: reservoir shoreline and marshlands.
> Havasu Reservoir provides essential wetland habitat for migratory waterfowl.
> Near Lake Havasu City.

Hells Canyon Phoenix BLM: 602-580-5500. Est. 1990.
> 9,900 acres: desert mountains and canyons.
> Peaks of the Hieroglyphic Range.
> Near Phoenix.

Hellsgate Tonto NF, 602-225-5200. Est. 1984.
> 37,440 acres: arid forest and canyons.
> The deep pools of Tonto and Haigler creeks make cool swimming holes.
> Near Payson.

Hummingbird Springs Phoenix BLM, 602-580-5500. Est. 1990.
> 31,200 acres: desert mountains.
> Features prominent Sugarloaf Mountain, 3,418 feet.
> Near Phoenix.

Imperial Imperial NWR, 520-783-3371. Est. 1990.
> 9,220 acres: riparian and desert areas.
> The Colorado River supports the rare Yuma clapper rail bird.
> Near Yuma.

Juniper Mesa Prescott NF, 520-771-4700. Est. 1984.
> 7,406 acres: arid forest mesa.
> Old-growth forest and views from the Juniper Mesa rim.
> Near Prescott.

Kachina Peaks Coconino NF, 520-526-0866. Est. 1984.
> 18,616 acres: arid mountain forest.
> 12,633-foot Humphrey's Peak, the highest point in Arizona.
> Near Flagstaff.

Kanab Creek Arizona Strip BLM, 435-688-3200 and Kaibab NF, 520-643-7395. Est. 1984.
6,700 acres (BLM) and 68,600 acres (NF): desert canyons.
Kanab Creek is the largest tributary canyon system on the north side of the Grand Canyon.
Near Fredonia.

Kendrich Mountain Kaibab NF, 800-863-0546. Est. 1984.
6,510 acres: arid mountain forest.
Features stands of old-growth pine important for deer and mountain lion habitat.
Near Williams.

Kofa Kofa NWR, 520-783-7861. Est. 1990.
516,200 acres: desert mountains.
Home of unique desert bighorn sheep and the California palm, the only native palm in Arizona.
Near Yuma.

Mazatzal Tonto NF, 602-225-5200. Est. 1964.
252,494 acres: arid mountain forest and desert.
Tremendous views as scrub desert turns to pine, walnut, and sycamore.
Near Payson.

Miller Peak Coronado NF, 520-670-4552. Est. 1984.
20,190 acres: desert mountain.
The 9,000-foot peak in the Huachucas Mountains is flanked by steep canyons and incredible vistas.
Near Sierra Vista.

Mount Baldy Apache NF, 520-333-4301. Est. 1970.
7,079 acres: mountain.
Above treeline, 11403-foot Mount Baldy is the second highest point in Arizona.
Near Springerville.

Mount Logan Arizona Strip BLM, 435-688-3200. Est. 1984.
 14,650 acres: desert canyon and arid forest.
 Unique volcanic remains and an eroded amphitheater known as Hells
  Hole.
 Near Colorado City.

Mount Nutt Kingman BLM, 520-692-4400. Est. 1990.
 27,660 acres: desert mountains.
 Sagebrush hills and mountains provide important desert bighorn sheep
  habitat.
 Near Kingman.

Mount Tipton Kingman BLM, 520-692-4400. Est. 1990.
 30,760 acres: desert mountain.
 Features the Cerbat Pinnacles, immense tusklike rows of maroon-
  colored spires.
 Near Kingman.

Mount Trumbull Arizona Strip BLM, 435-688-3200. Est. 1984.
 7,880 acres: desert mesa.
 Mount Trumbull is a large basalt-capped mesa.
 Near Colorado City.

Mount Wilson Kingman BLM, 520-692-4400. Est. 1990.
 23,900 acres: mountain desert.
 Eight-mile-long Wilson Ridge features 5,445-foot Mount Wilson.
 Near Kingman.

Mount Wrightson Coronado NF, 520-670-4552. Est. 1984.
 25,260 acres: mountain.
 Mount Wrightson at 9,450 feet is the highest peak in the Santa Rita
  Mountains.
 Near Tucson.

Muggins Mountain Yuma BLM, 520-317-3200. Est. 1990.
    7,711 acres: mountain desert.
    Deeply cut drainages dissect the rugged beauty of Muggins Mountain.
    Near Yuma.

Munds Mountain Coconino NF, 520-526-0866. Est. 1984.
    24,411 acres: arid forest and red rock.
    Munds Mountain is named after the original 19th century cow trail,
        now Schnebly Hill Road.
    Near Sedona.

Needles Eye Phoenix BLM, 602-580-5500. Est. 1990.
    8,760 acres: desert canyons and mountains.
    1,000-foot walls along the Gila River known as the Needles Eye.
    Tribal permits required.
    Near Globe. $

New Water Mountains Yuma BLM, 520-317-3200. Est. 1990.
    24,600 acres: desert mesas and canyons.
    New Water and Dripping Springs are important desert bighorn sheep
        lambing areas, contiguous with Kofa NWR.
    Near Yuma.

North Maricopa Mountains Phoenix BLM, 602-580-5500. Est. 1990.
    63,200 acres: desert mountain.
    Jumble of long ridges and isolated peaks separated by bajadas and
        washes.
    Near Phoenix.

North Santa Teresa Safford BLM, 520-348-4400. Est. 1990.
    5,800 acres: desert and volcanic plugs.
    A 1,000-foot-high, mile-long rhyolitic plug is known as Black Rock.
    Tribal permits required.
    Near Safford. $

Organ Pipe Cactus Organ Pipe Cactus NM, 520-387-6849. Est. 1978.
312,600 acres: Sonoran desert.
Features rare organ pipe cactus.
Near Ajo.

Paiute Arizona Strip BLM, 435-688-3200. Est. 1984.
87,900 acres: desert and arid mountain forest.
The Virgin Mountains feature 8,012-foot Mount Bangs.
Near St. George, Utah.

Pajarita Coronado NF, 520-670-4552. Est. 1984.
7,553 acres: desert canyons.
Pristine Sycamore Canyon.
Near Nogales.

Paria Canyon–Vermilion Cliffs Arizona Strip BLM, 435-688-3230.
Est. 1984.
132,400 acres (20,000 in Utah): desert canyons and cliffs.
Nationally known Paria Canyon has towering desert varnished walls
and red rock amphitheaters.
Near Page. $

Peloncillo Safford BLM, 520-348-4400. Est. 1990.
19,440 acres: desert mountains.
Rich archaeologic sites from the historic Butterfield Stage Route.
Near San Simon.

Petrified Forest Petrified Forest NP, 520-524-6228. Est. 1970.
50,260 acres: desert badlands.
World's largest, most colorful concentrations of petrified wood.
Near Holbrook.

Pine Mountain Prescott NF, 520-771-4700. Est. 1972.
20,061 acres: desert mountains and pine/juniper forest.
Also part of Tonto National Forest, it features an island of tall ponde
rosa pine along the high Verde River Rim.
Near Prescott.

Pusch Ridge Coronado NF, 520-670-4552. Est. 1978.
  56,933 acres: mountain and desert canyons.
  Features part of pristine Sycamore Canyon.
  Near Tucson.

Rawhide Mountains Lake Havasu BLM, 520-505-1200. Est. 1990.
  38,470 acres: desert canyons and outcrops.
  Bill Williams River (seasonal) flows through a 600-foot-deep gorge.
  Near Lake Havasu City.

Red Rock–Secret Mountain Coconino NF, 520-526-0866. Est. 1984.
  47,194 acres: desert canyons and mountains.
  Red bluffs and pristine Oak Creek Canyon.
  Near Flagstaff.

Redfield Canyon Safford BLM, 520-348-4400. Est. 1990.
  6,600 acres: desert canyons.
  Redfield Canyon is a narrow red-walled chasm.
  Near Benson.

Rincon Mountain Coronado NF, 520-670-4552. Est. 1984.
  38,590 acres: arid mountain forest and desert.
  Also referred to as Saguaro East, featuring spectacular cactus
      country views.
  Near Tucson.

Saddle Mountain Kaibab NF, 800-863-0546. Est. 1984.
  40,539 acres: desert canyon and arid forest.
  House Rock Valley supports a herd of bison.
  Near Fredonia.

Saguaro Saguaro NP, 520-733-5100. Est. 1976.
  71,400 acres: desert.
  Saguaro cactus, the state symbol of Arizona, survives despite
      vandalism and other threats.
  Near Tucson.

Salome Tonto NF, 602-225-5200. Est. 1984.
  18,531 acres: arid forest and desert canyon.
  Salome and Workman creeks harbor rainbow and brown trout.
  Near Globe.

Salt River Canyon Tonto NF, 602-225-5200. Est. 1984.
  32,101 acres: desert canyon.
  One of the most popular rafting and tubing destinations in Arizona.
  Near Phoenix.

Santa Teresa Coronado NF, 520-670-4552. Est. 1984.
  26,780 acres: desert and arid forest.
  Volcanic plugs and high spiritual mesas dominate the area.
  Tribal permits required.
  Near Safford. $

Sierra Ancha Tonto NF, 602-225-5200. Est. 1964.
  20,850 acres: arid forest and desert canyons.
  Deep canyons and ancient cliff dwellings.
  Near Globe.

Sierra Estrella Lower Gila BLM, 602-580-5500. Est. 1990.
  14,400 acres: desert mountains and canyons.
  Features knife-edged ridges, steep slopes, and rough rocky canyons.
  Near Phoenix.

Signal Mountain Lower Gila BLM, 602-580-5500. Est. 1990.
  13,350 acres: desert canyons and mountains.
  Features sharp volcanic peaks and steep-walled canyons.
  Near Phoenix.

South Maricopa Mountains Lower Gila BLM, 602-580-5500. Est. 1990.
  60,100 acres: desert mountains and plains.
  Extensive habitat for Sonoran desert plants.
  Near Phoenix.

Strawberry Crater Coconino NF, 520-526-0866. Est. 1984.
10,743 acres: desert lava beds.
Strawberrry Crater is the largest lava flow in the area.
Near Flagstaff.

Superstition Tonto NF, 602-225-5200. Est. 1964.
159,780 acres: arid mountain forest.
4,553-foot Weaver's Needle and Superstition Mountain are well-
known Phoenix landmarks.
Near Phoenix.

Swansea Lake Havasu BLM, 520-505-1200. Est. 1990.
16,400 acres: desert mountains.
Features the Buckskin Mountains and a portion of the Bill Williams
River.
Near Parker.

Sycamore Canyon Kaibab NF, 800-863-0546. Est. 1990.
55,942 acres: desert canyons.
Flourish of red rock buttes and sheer cliffs along Sycamore Creek.
Near Williams.

Table Top Lower Gila BLM, 602-580-5500. Est. 1990.
34,400 acres: desert mountains.
4,373-foot Table Top Mountain is a well-known Phoenix landmark;
supports saguaro and cholla cactus.
Near Phoenix.

Tres Alomos Kingman BLM, 602-692-4400. Est. 1990.
8,300 acres: desert canyons and mountains.
Joshua trees and creosote bush dot the landscape.
Near Kingman.

Trigo Mountains Yuma BLM, 520-317-3200. Est. 1990.
   30,300 acres: desert mountains.
   Heavily dissected by washes like Red Cloud Wash, Clip Wash, and
      Hart Mine Wash.
   Near Yuma.

Upper Burro Creek Kingman BLM, 602-692-4400. Est. 1990.
   7,440 acres: desert and perennial stream.
   Thirteen miles of clear-pooled Burro Creek.
   Near Kingman.

Wabayuma Peak Kingman BLM, 602-692-4400. Est. 1990.
   40,000 acres: desert mountain and arid forest.
   Dominated by 7,601-foot Wabayuma Peak.
   Near Kingman.

Warm Springs Kingman BLM, 602-692-4400. Est. 1990.
   112,400 acres: desert mesa.
   Warm Springs and other springs allow for extended camping trips.
   Near Kingman.

West Clear Creek Coconino NF, 520-526-0866. Est. 1984.
   15,238 acres: desert and riparian area.
   Beautiful Indian Maiden Falls.
   Near Prescott.

Wet Beaver Coconino NF, 520-526-0866. Est. 1984.
   6,155 acres: river canyon.
   Beaver Creek provides essential water for wildlife.
   Near Prescott.

White Canyon Phoenix BLM, 602-580-5500. Est. 1990.
   5,800 acres: desert canyon.
   White Canyon, numerous side canyons, and Rincon, a towering
      escarpment.
   Near Superior.

Woodchute Prescott NF, 602-771-4700. Est. 1984.
  5,833 acres: arid mountain forest.
  Ancient tree stumps and magnificent views of Verde Valley.
  Near Prescott.

Woolsey Peak Lower Gila BLM, 602-580-5500. Est. 1990.
  64,000 acres: desert mountain.
  Often grouped with Signal Peak, 3,270-foot Woolsey Peak rises above
    the Gila River.
  Near Phoenix.

ARKANSAS

Big Lake Big Lake NWR, 870-564-2429. Est. 1976.
  2,143 acres: shallow lake and wetlands.
  Important stop for migratory birds and bald eagles on the Lower
    Mississippi River.
  Near Manila.

Black Fork Mountain Ouachita NF, 501-321-5202. Est. 1984.
  13,579 acres (5,149 in Oklahoma): temperate mountain forest.
  Rock flows or screes dominate the ridge of 2,403-foot Black Fork
    Mountain.
  Near Page, Oklahoma.

Note: Within the Buffalo National River there are three wilderness areas: Upper Buffalo, Lower Buffalo, and Ponco.

Caney Creek Ouachita NF, 501-321-5202. Est. 1975.
  14,460 acres: creeks and temperate forest.
  Scenic Caney Creek, Short Creek, and sandstone rock outcrops.
  Near Mena.

Dry Creek Ouachita NF, 501-321-5202. Est. 1984.
  6,310 acres: temperate mountain forest.
  Features a vertical wall of rock called Chimney Rock and a few black
    bears.
  Near Boonesville.

East Fork Ozark NF, 501-284-3150. Est. 1984.
  10,688 acres: rolling temperate forest.
  Quality deer habitat.
  Near Hot Springs.

Flatside Ouachita NF, 501-321-5202. Est. 1984.
  9,507 acres: temperate mixed forest.
  Features Flatside Pinnacle, a 1,550-foot-high rock outcrop.
  Near Little Rock.

Hurricane Creek Ozark NF, 870-446-5122. Est. 1984.
  15,427 acres: temperate forest and creeks.
  A natural bridge and cool clear creeks.
  Near Pelsor.

Leatherwood Ozark NF, 870-269-3228. Est. 1984.
  16,980 acres: temperate forest and creeks.
  Contiguous with the Lower Buffalo; includes many caves and springs.
  Near Mountain View.

Lower Buffalo Buffalo NR, 870-741-5443. Est. 1978.
  22,500 acres: river and temperate forest.
  Buffalo W & SR and many scenic hollows and hills.
  Near Yellville.

Ponco Buffalo NR, 870-741-5443. Est. 1978.
  11,300 acres: river and temperate forest.
  Section of Buffalo W & SR includes the 500-foot cliff, Big Slurry.
  Near Jasper.

Poteau Mountain Ouachita NF, 501-321-5202. Est. 1984.
    11,299 acres: temperate mountain forest.
    2,406-foot Poteau Mountain; features several Norse "runestone"
        thought to be more than 900 years old.
    Near Waldron.

Richland Creek Ozark NF, 870-446-5122. Est. 1984.
    11,801 acres: temperate forest and creeks.
    Waterfalls, bluffs, and clear streams.
    Near Pelsor.

Upper Buffalo Buffalo NR, 870-741-5443. Est. 1984.
    12,035 acres: river and deciduous forest.
    Area includes bluffs along the Upper Buffalo W & SR, an entirely
        free-flowing river.
    Near Harrison.

CALIFORNIA

Ansel Adams Inyo/Sierra NF, 209-877-2218. Est. 1964.
    230,258 acres: granite mountains and forest.
    The Minarets Range's granite faces make for difficult climbing.
    Near Mammoth Lakes. $

Agua Tibia Cleveland NF, 619-673-6180. Est. 1975.
    15,933 acres: mixed mountain.
    Features mixed forest along diverse vegetation zones.
    Near Temecula. $

Argus Range Ridgecrest BLM, 760-384-5400. Est. 1994.
    74,890 acres: desert mountains.
    Several springs support desert bighorn sheep.
    Near Ridgecrest.

Big Maria Mountains Yuma BLM, 520-317-3200. Est. 1994.
    47,570 acres: desert mountains.
    Remote desert peaks.
    Near Blythe.

Bigelow Cholla Garden Needles BLM, 760-326-7000. Est. 1994.
    10,380 acres: desert mountains.
    The dark, volcanic Sacramento Mountains support Bigelow cholla
        cactus.
    Near Needles.

Bighorn Mountain Barstow BLM, 760-252-6000. Est. 1994.
    39,200 acres: desert mountains.
    Rugged, remote desert habitat for Joshua trees and Jeffrey pine.
    Near Barstow.

Black Mountain Barstow BLM, 760-252-6000. Est. 1994.
    13,940 acres: desert badlands.
    Black Mountain volcanic mesa.
    Near Ridgecrest.

Bright Star Ridgecrest BLM, 760-384-5400. Est. 1994.
    9,520 acres: arid forest.
    Granite mountains provide habitat for pinyon pine and juniper to
        Joshua tree forests.
    Near Bakersfield.

Bristol Mountains Needles BLM, 760-326-7000. Est. 1994.
    68,515 acres: desert mountains.
    Remote waterless mountains and volcanic plains.
    Near Needles.

Bucks Lake Plumas NF, 530-283-0555. Est. 1984.
    24,023 acres: forested basin and rock.
    Steep cliffs, glacial tarns, and 7,000-foot peaks like Mount Pleasant.
    Near Beckwourth.

Cadiz Dunes Needles BLM, 760-326-7000. Est. 1994.
   39,740 acres: desert dunes.
   Interdune habitat for Russian thistle.
   Near Twentynine Palms.

Caribou Lassen NF, 530-257-2151. Est. 1964.
   20,546 acres: temperate mountain forest.
   Lassen Trail and 7,000-foot Caribou Peaks highlight these volcanic
      mountains.
   Near Susanville.

Carrizo Gorge El Centro BLM, 760-337-4400. Est. 1994.
   15,700 acres: desert.
   Carrizo Gorge Trestle of the old San Diego–Arizona Railway.
   Near El Centro.

Carson-Iceberg Stanislaus NF, 209-795-1381. Est. 1984.
   161,501 acres: temperate mountain forest.
   A distinctive volcanic formation called "The Iceberg."
   Near Sonora. $

Castle Crags Shasta-Trinity NF, 530-235-2684. Est. 1984.
   11,048 acres: granite spires and temperate forest.
   Features the nearby Sacramento River and a section of the PCT.
   Near Castella.

Chanchelvilla Shasta-Trinity NF, 530-352-4211. Est. 1984.
   8,200 acres: mountain forest.
   Remote; receives few visitors.
   Near Deerlick Springs.

Chemehuevi Mountains Needles BLM, 760-326-7000. Est. 1994.
   64,320 acres: desert mountains.
   Scenic mountains along the Colorado River; habitat for many small
      desert mammals.
   Near Needles.

Chimney Peak Bakersfield BLM, 805-391-6000. Est. 1994.
13,700 acres: desert and granite mountains.
The old wagon route, the Sacatar Trail, crosses the area.
Near Ridgecrest.

Chuckwalla Mountains California Desert BLM, 909-697-5200.
Est. 1994.
158,950 acres: desert.
Crucial habitat for the desert tortoise.
Near Riverside.

Chumash Los Padres NF, 805-683-6711. Est. 1992.
38,200 acres: desert mountains.
Near the infamous San Andreas fault.
Near Los Bakersfield.

Cleghorn Lakes Barstow BLM, 760-252-6000. Est. 1994.
34,380 acres: desert.
Yucca and barrel cactus.
Near Palm Springs.

Clipper Mountains Needles BLM, 760-326-7000. Est. 1994.
40,000 acres: desert mountains.
Wild and remote landscape.
Near Needles.

Coso Range Ridgecrest BLM, 760-384-5400. Est. 1994.
50,520 acres: desert mountains.
Range supports intact stands of Joshua trees.
Near Ridgecrest.

Coyote Mountains El Centro BLM, 760-337-4400. Est. 1994.
17,000 acres: desert mountains.
Wind caves in sandblasted granite.
Near El Centro.

Cucamonga Angeles NF, 626-574-1613. Est. 1964.
   12,781 acres: temperate mountain forest.
   Features 8,859-foot Cucamonga Peak in the San Gabriel Mountains.
   Near Los Angeles. 🥾 $

Darwin Falls Ridgecrest BLM, 760-384-5400. Est. 1994.
   8,600 acres: desert canyon and creeks.
   Death Valley's Darwin Falls creates a lush oasis nearby, but is not part
      of the wilderness.
   Near Ridgecrest. 🥾

Dead Mountains Needles BLM, 726-326-7000. Est. 1994.
   48,850 acres: desert mountains.
   Jagged, steep, rust-colored Dead Mountains ridge.
   Near Needles. 🥾

Death Valley Death Valley NP, 760-786-2331. Est. 1994.
   3.16 million acres: desert basin and mountains.
   282-foot Badwater is the lowest elevation in the western hemisphere.
   Near Ridgecrest. 🥾 $

Desolation Eldorado NF, 530-644-6048. Est. 1969.
   63,475 acres: temperate mountain forest.
   Incredibly scenic; the area is heavily used.
   Near Camino. 🥾 $

Dick Smith Los Padres NF, 805-683-6711. Est. 1984.
   68,000 acres: arid mountain forest.
   Crucial habitat for deer and mountain lions.
   Near Santa Barbara. 🥾 〜

Dinkey Lakes Sierra NF, 209-855-8321. Est. 1984.
   30,000 acres: subalpine mountain forest.
   Adjacent to John Muir Wilderness; contains stands of ancient fir and
      pine.
   Near Huntington Lake. 🥾 $

Domeland Bakersfield BLM, 805-391-6000. Est. 1964.
> 130,161 acres: arid mountain forest.
> Features a section of the South Fork of the Kern W & SR.
> Near Ridgecrest.

El Paso Mountains Ridgecrest BLM, 760-384-5400. Est. 1994.
> 23,780 acres: desert badlands.
> Red buttes and dark, uplifted mesas.
> Near Ridgecrest.

Emigrant Stanislaus NF, 209-965-3434. Est. 1975.
> 112,338 acres: forest and alpine areas.
> Volcanic ridges and plugs highlight this Yosemite neighbor.
> Near Sonora.

Farallon San Francisco Bay NWR, 510-792-0222. Est. 1974.
> 141 acres: islands.
> Northern fur seals breed on Farallon Islands; closed to public
>> visitation.
> Near San Francisco.

Fish Creek Mountains El Centro BLM, 760-337-4400. Est. 1994.
> 25,940 acres: desert mountains.
> Great plateau rising above the desert basin with rugged ridges, peaks,
>> and twisted canyons.
> Near El Centro.

Funeral Mountains Death Valley NP, 760-786-2331. Est. 1994.
> 28,110 acres: desert mountains.
> Historic remnants from mining.
> Near Death Valley.

Garcia Los Padres NF, 805-683-6711. Est. 1992.
> 14,100 acres: arid mountain forest.
> Prolific wildflower blooms in spring.
> Near Goleta.

Golden Trout Sequoia NF, 209-784-1500. Est. 1978.
  305,464 acres: alpine and mountain forest.
  Home to native little kern golden trout.
  Near Lone Pine. $

Golden Valley Ridgecrest BLM, 760-384-5400. Est. 1994.
  37,700 acres: desert valley.
  Known for spectacular spring wildflowers.
  Near Ridgecrest.

Granite Chief Tahoe NF, 530-367-2224. Est. 1984.
  25,748 acres: alpine and mountain forest.
  Headwaters of the American W & SR.
  Near Truckee.

Grass Valley Ridgecrest BLM, 760-384-5400. Est. 1994.
  31,695 acres: desert basin.
  Habitat for the Mojave Desert ground squirrel.
  Near Ridgecrest.

Hauser Cleveland NF, 619-673-6180. Est. 1984.
  8,091 acres: arid forest and desert.
  A section of the PCT and scenic Salazar and Boneyard canyons.
  Near San Diego. $

Havasu Havasu NWR, 760-326-3853. Est. 1994.
  3,195 acres: lakeside desert and wetlands.
  The Colorado River and dammed backwaters provide feeding grounds
      for migratory waterfowl.
  Near Needles.

Hollow Hills Barstow BLM, 760-252-6000. Est. 1994.
  22,240 acres: desert hills.
  A gentle bajada laced with washes and low rolling ridges and peaks;
      home to the fringe-toed lizard.
  Near Baker.

Hoover Toiyabe NF, 702-932-7070. Est. 1964.
    48,622 acres: alpine and mountain forest.
    This Yosemite neighbor holds jagged peaks and lush meadows.
    Near Bridgeport.

Ibex Barstow BLM, 760-252-6000. Est. 1994.
    26,460 acres: desert.
    These sage hills offer Mojave Desert views.
    Near Death Valley.

Imperial (*see* Arizona).

Indian Pass El Centro BLM, 760-337-4400. Est. 1994.
    33,855 acres: desert mountains.
    Area threatened by the Glamis Gold Mine.
    Near El Centro.

Inyo Mountains Ridgecrest BLM, 760-384-5400. Est. 1994.
    205,020 acres: mountain forest.
    Keynote Peak highlights this Owens Valley landmark.
    Near Lone Pine.

Ishi Lassen NF, 530-257-2151. Est. 1984.
    42,866 acres: arid foothill forest.
    Ishi was the last man of the now extinct Yahi Yana tribe of these
        volcanic pillars and canyons.
    Near Chico.

Jacumba Mountains El Centro BLM, 760-337-4400. Est. 1994.
    33,670 acres: desert mountains.
    Dry, rugged habitat for desert animals.
    Near Jacumba.

Jennie Lakes Sequoia NF, 209-338-2251. Est. 1984.
  10,289 acres: alpine and mountain forest.
  Features 10,265-foot Mitchell Peak.
  Near Dunlap.

John Muir Sierra NF, 209-855-5360. Est. 1964.
  581,143 acres: alpine and mountain forest.
  14,000-foot-high peaks, canyons, meadows, and many streams and
    lakes.
  Near Mono Lake. $

Joshua Tree Joshua Tree NP, 760-367-5500. Est. 1976.
  561,470 acres: desert.
  Unique transition desert ecosystem supports cholla cactus,
    creosote, and Joshua trees.
  Near Indio. $

Kaiser Sierra NF, 209-855-5360. Est. 1976.
  22,700 acres: alpine and mountain forest.
  Popular mountain lakes and alpine ridges.
  Near Shaver Lake. $

Kelso Dunes Needles BLM, 760-326-7000. Est. 1994.
  129,580 acres: desert dunes.
  The stark Bristol Mountains offer a challenge for even the most
    experienced desert hiker. Nearby is Kelso Dunes National Pre-
    serve.
  Near Needles.

Kiavah Ridgecrest BLM, 760-384-5400. Est. 1994.
  88,290 acres: arid forest and desert.
  Transition zone between Sierras and the Mojave Desert.
  Near Ridgecrest.

Kingston Range Needles BLM, 760-326-7000. Est. 1994.
209,608 acres: desert mountains.
7,300-foot Kingston Peak, an island in a sea of desert lowland.
Near Baker. 🥾

Lassen Volcanic Lassen NP, 530-595-4444. Est. 1996.
78,982 acres: alpine and mountain forest.
10,457-foot Lassen is one of the most climbed volcanoes in the world.
Near Mineral. 🥾 ⬭ $

Lava Beds Lava Beds NM, 530-667-2282. Est. 1972.
28,460 acres: caves and volcanic formations.
The Modoc Indians used the lava flows for protection against the
    U.S. Army.
Near Tulelake. 🥾 ⬭ $

Little Chuckwalla Mountains Palm Springs BLM, 760-251-4800.
    Est. 1994.
28,880 acres: desert mountains.
Blooming Parry's nolina.
Near Blythe. 🥾

Little Picacho El Centro BLM, 760-337-4400. Est. 1994.
33,600 acres: desert mountains.
Habitat for wild burros, desert tortoises, and spotted bats.
Near El Centro. 🥾 ⬭

Machesna Mountain Los Padres NF, 805-925-9538. Est. 1984.
20,000 acres: arid mountain forest.
Healthy pine forest communities.
Near Santa Maria. 🥾 $

Malpais Mesa Ridgecrest BLM, 760-384-5400. Est. 1994.
32,360 acres: desert mesas and canyons.
Vegetation ranges from desert shrubs and grasses to pine and juniper
    forests.
Near Olancha. 🥾

Manley Peak Ridgecrest BLM, 760-384-5400. Est. 1994.
   16,105 acres: desert ridges and canyons.
   Springs support desert willow, cottonwood, and desert bighorn sheep.
   Near Ridgecrest.

Matilija Los Padres NF, 805-683-6711. Est. 1992.
   29,600 acres: arid mountain forest.
   Dry canyons and streambeds support the perennial "Matilrya poppy,"
      which grows up to seven feet tall.
   Near Santa Barbara.

Marble Mountain Klamath NF, 530-468-5351. Est. 1964.
   242,464 acres: temperate mountain forest.
   Features the PCT and nearly 100 lakes.
   Near Yreka.

Mecca Hills Palm Springs BLM, 760-251-4800. Est. 1994.
   24,200 acres: desert.
   Spectacular red and tan sedimentary badlands.
   Near Palm Springs.

Mesquite Needles BLM, 760-326-7000. Est. 1994.
   47,330 acres: desert mountains.
   Supports creosote brush sage, bajadas, blackbrush, and Joshua trees.
   Near Baker.

Mojave Mojave NP, 760-255-8801. Est. 1994.
   694,000 acres: desert.
   Founded in 1994; it includes Kelso Sand Dunes and historic Kelso
      Depot.
   Near Needles. $

Mokelumne Eldorado NF, 530-644-6048. Est. 1964.
   100,848 acres: subalpine and mountain forest.
   Deep granite-flanked Mokelumne River Canyon.
   Near Jackson. $

Monarch Sequoia NF, 209-338-2251. Est. 1984.
44,876 acres: mountain forest.
Includes geologically unique areas like 11,077-foot Hogback Peak.
Near Dunlap.

Mount Shasta Shasta-Trinity NF, 530-926-4511. Est. 1984.
37,710 acres: alpine and temperate mountain forest.
14,162-foot Mount Shasta dominates this heavily used wilderness.
Near McCloud. $

Newberry Mountains Barstow BLM, 760-252-6000. Est. 1994.
22,900 acres: desert mountains.
Home to rare cactus and other precious desert plants.
Near Needles.

Nopah Range Barstow BLM, 760-252-6000. Est. 1994.
10,860 acres: desert cliffs.
Harsh rocky landscape provides many ancient fossils.
Near Baker.

North Algodones Dunes El Centro BLM, 760-337-4400. Est. 1994.
32,240 acres: desert.
The 1,000-square-mile Algodones Sand Dune complex is one of the
largest in North America.
Near El Centro.

North Fork Six Rivers NF, 707-574-6233. Est. 1984.
8,100 acres: arid mountain forest and river.
Features the North Fork of the Eel W & SR; important winter
habitat for grazing wildlife.
Near Bridgeville.

North Mesquite Mountains Needles BLM, 760-326-7000. Est. 1994.
  25,540 acres: desert mountains.
  Joshua tree woodlands, yucca, cactus, and blackbrush.
  Near Baker.

Old Woman Mountains Needles BLM, 760-326-7000. Est. 1994.
  146,070 acres: desert mountains.
  "One woman, many mountains," is how locals describe the massive
      Old Woman Mountains.
  Near Needles.

Orocopia Mountains Palm Springs BLM, 760-251-4800. Est. 1994.
  40,735 acres: desert mountains.
  Steep desert climbs to Orocopia Peak.
  Near Indio.

Owens Peak Ridgecrest BLM, 760-384-5400. Est. 1994.
  74,640 acres: mountains and desert canyons.
  Spring wildflowers of Short Canyon.
  Near Ridgecrest.

Pahrump Valley Barstow BLM, 760-252-6000. Est. 1994.
  74,800 acres: desert mountains.
  Rugged desert wilds.
  Near Baker.

Palen-McCoy Palm Springs BLM, 760-251-4800. Est. 1994.
  270,629 acres: mountain desert.
  Five distinct mountain ranges separated by broad bajadas.
  Near Blythe.

Palo Verde Mountains El Centro BLM, 760-337-4400. Est. 1994.
  32,310 acres: desert mountains.
  Supports stands of paloverde, mesquite, and ironwood.
  Near Blythe.

Phillip Burton Point Reyes NS, 415-663-1092. Est. 1992.
   25,370 acres: coastal forest, breakers, and grassy hills.
   More than 45 percent of all bird species in North America have been
      sighted here.
   Near San Fransisco.

Picacho Peak El Centro BLM, 760-337-4400. Est. 1994.
   7,700 acres: desert mountains.
   Rock "tinajas" and dry waterfalls.
   Near El Centro.

Pine Creek Cleveland NF, 619-445-6235. Est. 1984.
   13,686 acres: arid forest and desert.
   Wildlife habitat is threatened by trash from illegal border crossing.
   Near San Diego.

Pinnacles Pinnacles NM, 408-389-4485. Est. 1976.
   12,952 acres: desert.
   Spirelike rock formations from 500 to 1,200 feet high with caves and
      volcanic features.
   Near Paicines. $

Piper Mountain Ridgecrest BLM, 760-384-5400. Est. 1994.
   72,600 acres: desert and arid forest.
   Next to Death Valley; alluvial fans cover large portions of the area.
   Near Bishop.

Piute Mountains Needles BLM, 760-326-7000. Est. 1994.
   36,840 acres: desert mountains.
   The sacred "kwikantsoka" mountains of Mohave Indians.
   Near Needles.

Point Reyes (*see* Phillip Burton).

Red Buttes Rogue River NF, 541-482-3333. Est. 1984.
  19,900 acres (3,750 in Oregon): mountain forest.
  The high iron and magnesium content brightens the buttes; partially
    in Oregon.
  Near Yreka.

Resting Spring Range Barstow BLM, 760-252-6000. Est. 1994.
  78,868 acres: desert mountains.
  Home to the rare spring-loving century plant.
  Near Barstow.

Rice Valley Palm Springs BLM, 760-251-4800. Est. 1994.
  40,820 acres: desert.
  Features Rice Valley Sand Dunes.
  Near Vidal Junction.

Riverside Mountains Palm Springs BLM, 760-251-4800. Est. 1994.
  22,380 acres: desert mountains.
  Mountains feature rugged rock ledges.
  Near Vidal Junction.

Rodman Mountains Barstow BLM, 760-252-6000. Est. 1994.
  27,700 acres: desert mountains.
  Excellent petroglyphs.
  Near Barstow.

Russian Klamath NF, 530-468-5351. Est. 1984.
  12,000 acres: mountain forest.
  Rough, wild country with lakes, streams, and mountains.
  Near Fort Jones.

Sacatar Trail Ridgecrest BLM, 760-384-5400. Est. 1994.
  51,900 acres: desert and arid mountain forest.
  Historic eastern Sierra wagon road, Sacatar Trail.
  Near Ridgecrest.

Saddle Peak Hills Barstow BLM, 760-252-6000. Est. 1994.
1,440 acres: desert.
These less-visited hills offer untrammeled exploration.
Near Baker.

San Gabriel Angeles NF, 626-335-1251. Est. 1968.
36,118 acres: arid forest and desert mountains.
Excellent views of Palomar Mountain.
Near Arcadia. 🥾

*Note: There are two separate San Gorgonio Wilderness areas. One
established in 1964 by the original Wilderness Act and the other created in 1994 by the California Desert Protection Act.*

San Gorgonio Palm Springs BLM, 760-251-4800. Est. 1994.
37,980 acres: dry hills and canyons.
Steep, rugged mountains; unique transition zones between desert,
coastal, and mountain environments.
Near Palm Springs. 🥾

San Gorgonio San Bernardino NF, 909-794-1123. Est. 1964.
96,649 acres: arid mountain forest.
Many peaks over 10,000 feet and views of Los Angeles.
Near Los Angeles. 🥾 ∪

San Jacinto San Bernardino NF, 909-659-2117. Est. 1964.
33,408 acres: arid mountain forest.
Waterfalls and 10,804-foot San Jacinto Peak.
Near Palm Springs. 🥾 ◯

San Mateo Canyon Cleveland NF, 909-736-1811. Est. 1984.
39,540 acres: arid forest and canyon.
Canyon and streamside habitat for the rare ocellated humboldt lily.
Near Corona. 🥾 $

San Rafael Los Padres NF, 805-925-9538. Est. 1968.
  197,570 acres: arid mountain forest.
  Scenic Sierra Madre Mountains.
  Near Santa Maria.

Santa Lucia Los Padres NF, 805-925-9538. Est. 1978.
  21,704 acres: arid mountain forest.
  Scenic Lopez Canyon and several waterfalls.
  Near Santa Maria.

Santa Rosa San Bernardino NF, 909-659-2117. Est. 1984.
  84,143 acres: arid forest and desert canyons.
  Crucial mountain lion and bighorn sheep habitat.
  Near Santa Rosa.

Santa Rosa Mountains Palm Springs BLM, 760-251-4800. Est. 1994.
  64,340 acres: desert mountains.
  Mountains rise 7,000 feet above sea level to provide important
    bighorn sheep habitat.
  Near Palm Springs.

Sawtooth Mountains El Centro BLM, 760-337-4400. Est. 1994.
  35,080 acres: dry ridges.
  Surrounded by Anza-Borrego Desert State Park and habitat for desert
    bighorn sheep; access limited.
  Near Borrego Springs and San Diego.

Sequoia–Kings Canyon Sequoia–Kings Canyon NP, 209-565-3708.
    Est. 1984.
  219,700 acres: mountain forest and alpine.
  Features four of the world's largest sequoias.
  Near Lone Pine. $

Sheep Hole Valley Needles BLM, 760-326-7000. Est. 1994.
174,800 acres: desert basin.
Large valley and basin inhabited by desert tortoise and other wildlife.
Near Twentynine Palms.

Sespe Los Padres NF, 805-245-3731. Est. 1992.
219,700 acres: mountain forest.
Known for extreme whitewater and Sespe Hot Springs..
Near Frazier Park.

Sheep Mountain Angeles NF, 626-574-1613. Est. 1984.
42,367 acres: arid mountain forest.
Features 10,064-foot Mount Baldy.
Near Los Angeles.

Silver Peak Los Padres NF, 408-385-5434. Est. 1992.
14,500 acres: mountain forest.
Several creeks provide riparian habitat for deer and other mammals.
Near San Miguel.

Siskiyou Klamath NF, 530-493-2243. Est. 1984.
153,000 acres: mountain forest.
Upper south fork of the Smith W & SR.
Near Happy Camp.

Snow Mountain Mendocino NF, 530-963-3128. Est. 1984.
37,000 acres: alpine and mountain forest.
Snow from this broad mountain drains to the Sacramento and Eel
rivers.
Near Upper Lake.

South Nopah Range Barstow BLM, 760-252-6000. Est. 1994.
16,780 acres: rolling desert slopes.
Home to prairie falcons and the ivory-spined agave plant.
Near Barstow.

South Sierra Inyo NF, 760-876-6200. Est. 1984.
  60,324 acres: alpine and mountain forest.
  Features a section of the PCT.
  Near Lone Pine. 🥾 ⚓ $

South Warner Modoc NF, 530-279-6116. Est. 1964.
  70,729 acres: arid mountain forest.
  Scenic Blue Lake.
  Near Cedarville. 🥾

Stateline Needles BLM, 760-326-7000. Est. 1994.
  7,050 acres: desert mountains.
  On the border with Nevada are the rocky, isolated Clark Mountains.
  Near Needles.

Stepladder Mountains Needles BLM, 760-326-7000. Est. 1994.
  81,600 acres: desert mountains.
  Bajadas and washes provide habitat for desert tortoise and bighorn
    sheep.
  Near Needles.

Surprise Canyon Ridgecrest BLM, 760-384-5400. Est. 1994.
  29,180 acres: desert canyon.
  Rocky canyon walls support the endangered panamint daisy.
  Near Ridgecrest. 🥾

Sylvania Mountains Ridgecrest BLM, 760-384-5400. Est. 1994.
  17,820 acres: desert hills and mountains.
  Vast views of Last Chance Range, Piper Mountain, and Fish Lake
    Valley.
  Near Bishop. 🥾

Thousand Lakes Lassen NF, 530-336-5521. Est. 1964.
  16,335 acres: alpine and mountain forest.
  Many lakes and molten lava mud pots.
  Near Susanville. 🥾 ⚓ $

Trilobite Needles BLM, 760-326-7000. Est. 1994.
    33,270 acres: desert mountains.
    Rugged Marble Mountains, many fossils, and non-commercial
       rockhounding.
    Near Ludlow.

Trinity Alps Shasta-Trinity NF, 530-623-2121. Est. 1984.
    513,100 acres: alpine and mountain forest.
    Many lakes and streams offer excellent alpine fishing opportunities.
    Near Weaverville. $

Turtle Mountains Needles BLM, 760-326-7000. Est. 1994.
    144,500 acres: desert peaks and spires.
    Features 3,675-foot Mopah Peak, a weathered volcanic pinnacle.
    Near Needles.

Ventana Los Padres NF, 408-385-5434. Est. 1992.
    205,489 acres: mountain forest.
    Redwoods and shade-seeking ferns.
    Near Big Sur.

Whipple Mountains Needles BLM, 760-326-7000. Est. 1994.
    77,520 acres: desert mountains.
    Striking brick red volcanic formations.
    Near Parker.

Yolla Bolly–Middle Eel Mendocino NF, 530-824-5196. Est. 1964.
    151,626 acres: alpine and mountain forest.
    "Yo-la Bo-li" means snow-covered high peak; also the headwaters of
       the Eel W & SR.
    Near Corning. $

Yosemite Yosemite NP, 209-372-0200. Est. 1964.
  677,600 acres: rock domes and mountain forest.
  Giant sequoias and the glacially carved cliffs of famous Yosemite Valley.
  Near Yosemite Village. 🥾 ⚓ 🔦 $

COLORADO

Black Canyon of the Gunnison Black Canyon of the Gunnison NM,
    970-249-1915. Est. 1976.
  11,180 acres: arid canyon.
  Features deep scoured canyon walls of Proterzoic crystalline rock.
  Near Gunnison. 🥾 ⚓ 🔦 $

Buffalo Peaks Pike NF, 719-836-2031. Est. 1993.
  43,410 acres: arid forest and mountains.
  Mountain meadows are habitat for elk, deer, and mountain lions.
  Near Fairplay. 🥾

Byers Peak Arapaho-Roosevelt NF, 970-877-4100. Est. 1993.
  8,095 acres: alpine and mountain forest.
  Subalpine fir and bristlecone forests highlight these 12,000-foot
    mountains.
  Near Winter Park. 🥾

Cache La Poudre Arapaho-Roosevelt NF, 970-498-2775. Est. 1980.
  9,308 acres: arid forest and river.
  Features the Cache La Poudre W & SR.
  Near Fort Collins. 🥾 ⚓

Collegiate Peaks San Isabel NF, 719-539-3591. Est. 1980.
  167,996 acres: alpine forest.
  Multiple 14,000-foot peaks in this popular wilderness.
  Near Leadville. 🥾 🔦

Comanche Peak Arapaho-Roosevelt NF, 970-498-2775. Est. 1980.
66,901 acres: mountain forest.
Mountain meadows and alpine vistas, with good elk habitat.
Near Fort Collins.

Eagles Nest Arapaho-Roosevelt NF, 970-468-5400. Est. 1976.
13,496 acres: alpine and mountain forest.
Includes 17 peaks over 13,000 feet.
Near Glenwood Springs.

Flat Tops White River NF, 970-878-4039. Est. 1975.
235,230 acres: alpine and mountain forest.
Many plateau lakes harbor cutthroat trout.
Near Glenwood Springs.

Fossil Ridge Gunnison NF, 970-641-0471. Est. 1993.
33,060 acres: alpine and mountain forest.
Eroded sandstone ridge and rock garden.
Near Gunnison.

Great Sand Dunes Great Sand Dune NM, 719-378-2312. Est. 1976.
33,450 acres: desert and arid forest.
North America's tallest dunes at 700 feet.
Near Alamosa. $

Greenhorn Mountain San Isabel NF, 719-269-8500. Est. 1993.
22,040 acres: dry mountain forest.
Unique "island" mountain range not attached to Rocky Mountains.
Near Canon City.

Holy Cross White River NF, 970-827-5715. Est. 1980.
123,410 acres: mountain forest.
Prominent 14,005-foot Mount of the Holy Cross.
Near Minturn.

Hunter-Fryingpan White River NF, 970-963-2266. Est. 1993.
  82,929 acres: river and mountain forest.
  Famous fishing in the Fryingpan River.
  Near Glenwood Springs.

Indian Peaks Arapaho-Roosevelt NF, 970-887-4100. Est. 1978.
  73,391 acres: alpine and mountain forest.
  Heavily used area next to Rocky Mountain National Park.
  Near Granby. $

La Garita Gunnison NF, 970-641-0471. Est. 1980.
  129,626 acres: alpine and mountain forest.
  Features 14,000-foot San Louis Peak and a section of the CDT.
  Near Gunnison.

Lizard Head San Juan NF, 970-882-7296. Est. 1980.
  41,496 acres: alpine and mountain forest.
  Multiple fourteeners in the San Miguel Mountains.
  Near Telluride. $

Lost Creek Pike NF, 303-275-5610. Est. 1980.
  120,151 acres: mountain forest.
  Granite uplift creates intriguing rocky terrain.
  Near Woodland Park.

Maroon Bells–Snowmass White River NF, 970-925-3445. Est. 1980.
  183,847 acres: alpine and mountain forest.
  Heavily used wilderness that includes Crater Lake.
  Near Aspen.

Mesa Verde Mesa Verde NP, 970-529-4461. Est. 1976.
  8,100 acres: dry mesa and cliffs.
  Ancient cliff dwellings of the Ancestral Pueblo people.
  Near Cortez. $

Mount Evans Arapaho-Roosevelt NF, 303-275-5610. Est. 1980.
74,401 acres: alpine and mountain forest.
Highest paved automobile road in North America that reaches the
summit of Mount Evans.
Near Idaho Springs.

Mount Massive San Isabel NF, 719-486-0749. Est. 1980.
30,607 acres: alpine and mountain forest.
Mount Massive has most area above 14,000 feet in continental United
States.
Near Leadville.

Mount Sneffels Uncompahgre NF, 970-240-5300. Est. 1980.
16,587 acres: alpine and mountain forest.
Blue Lakes enrich a Mount Sneffels adventure.
Near Ouray.

Mount Zirkel Routt NF, 970-879-1870. Est. 1964.
160,648 acres: alpine and mountain forest.
Many good lakes for high-country fishing.
Near Steamboat Springs.

Neota Arapaho-Roosevelt NF, 970-498-2775. Est. 1980.
9,924 acres: alpine and mountain forest.
Flat-top ridges formed by erosion and glacial action.
Near Fort Collins.

Never Summer Arapaho-Roosevelt NF, 970-887-4100. Est. 1980.
21,090 acres: alpine and mountain forest.
Peaks with names like Stratus, Cumulus, and Nimbus.
Near Grand Lake. $

Platte River (*see* Wyoming).

Powderhorn Gunnison NF, 970-641-0471. Est. 1993.
   61,714 acres: mountain forest and grassland.
   Meadows and aspen groves provide habitat for elk, deer, and other
      wildlife.
   Near Gunnison. ✓

Ptarmigan Peak Arapaho-Roosevelt NF, 970-468-5400. Est. 1993.
   13,175 acres: mountain forest.
   Features 11,773-foot Ptarmigan Peak.
   Near Fraser. 👢

Raggeds Gunnison NF, 970-641-0471. Est. 1980.
   65,430 acres: mountain forest.
   Excellent horse-packing through aspen and spruce forests.
   Near Gunnison. 👢

Rawah Arapaho-Roosevelt NF, 970-498-1100. Est. 1964.
   73,934 acres: alpine and mountain forest.
   Stark granite of Rawah Peaks.
   Near Walden. 👢 ✓ ◊

Sangre De Cristo San Isabel NF, 719-269-8500. Est. 1993.
   226,455 acres: mountain forest.
   Heavy populations of elk.
   Near Saguache. 👢

Sarvis Creek Routt NF, 970-879-1722. Est. 1993.
   47,140 acres: mountain forest.
   Watershed for the Yampa River.
   Near Steamboat Springs. 👢 ✓

South San Juan Rio Grande NF, 719-274-8971. Est. 1980.
   158,790 acres: alpine and mountain forest.
   High-alpine lakes and meadows.
   Near Pagosa Springs.

Uncompahgre Uncompahgre NF, 970-240-5300. Est. 1980.
   99,399 acres: alpine and mountain forest.
   Rocky summits, aspen groves, and abundant wildlife.
   Near Lake City.

Vasquez Peak Arapaho-Roosevelt NF, 970-887-4100. Est. 1993.
   12,300 acres: alpine and mountain forest.
   Includes a section of the CDT.
   Near Fraser.

Weminuche San Juan NF, 970-247-4874. Est. 1975.
   492,418 acres: alpine and mountain forest.
   An average elevation of 10,500 feet makes these San Juan Mountains
      the highest range in North America.
   Near Durango.

West Elk Gunnison NF, 970-641-0471. Est. 1964.
   176,412 acres: alpine and mountain forest.
   Popular getaway for horse packers and hunters.
   Near Gunnison.

FLORIDA

Alexander Springs Ocala NF, 352-669-3522. Est. 1984.
   7,941 acres: wetland and forest.
   The springs produce 80 million gallons of freshwater each day.
   Near Altoona.

Big Gum Swamp Osceola NF, 904-752-2577. Est. 1984.
   13,660 acres: wetland and forest.
   Old-growth cypress-gum forest.
   Near Olustee.

Billies Bay Ocala NF, 352-669-3153. Est. 1984.
   3,092 acres: wetland forest.
   Bay harbors catfish and silver perch.
   Near Silver Springs.

Bradwell Bay Apalachicola NF, 850-926-3561. Est. 1975.
   24,602 acres: wetland forest.
   Home to bobcats, otters, woodpeckers, and many
      songbirds.
   Near Crawfordville.

Cedar Keys Lower Suwannee NWR, 352-493-0238. Est. 1972.
   379 acres: island wetlands.
   Home to many birds, including ospreys, pelicans, and
      great blue herons.
   Near Cedar Keys.

Chassahowitzka Chassahowitz NWR, 352-563-2088. Est. 1976.
   23,580 acres: coastal wetland.
   These estuaries and hardwood swamps support many threatened
      reptiles.
   Near Crystal River.

Everglades Everglades NP, 305-242-7700. Est. 1978.
   1.3 million acres: wetland and forest.
   Largest remaining subtropical wilderness in the United States.
   Near Homestead. $

*Note: Great White Heron, National Key Deer, and Key West wilderness
   areas describe the area formerly referred to as Florida Keys Wilderness.*

Great White Heron National Key Deer NWR, 305-872-2239. Est. 1975.
   1,900 acres: wetland forest.
   Critical habitat for herons and other waterfowl.
   Near Big Pine Key.

Island Bay J. N. "Ding" Darling NWR, 941-472-1100. Est. 1970.
   20 acres: island wetland.
   Home to nesting pelicans.
   Near Sanibel.

J. N. "Ding" Darling J. N. "Ding" Darling NWR, 941-472-1100.
   Est. 1976.
   2,619 acres: island beach and wetland.
   Named after the famous federal duck stamp artist.
   Near Sanibel.

Juniper Prairie Ocala NF, 352-625-2520. Est. 1984.
   14,281 acres: wetland forest.
   Unique semitropical scenery.
   Near Silver Springs. $

Key West National Key Deer NWR, 305-872-2239. Est. 1975.
   2,019 acres: wetland forest.
   Habitat includes fringe and scrub mangrove wetlands, hardwood ham
      mocks, and salt marsh.
   Near Big Pine Key.

Lake Woodruff Lake Woodruff NWR, 904-985-4673. Est. 1976.
   1,066 acres: lake wetland.
   Crucial habitat for endangered wood storks, snail kite, and West
      Indian manatee.
   Near DeLeon Springs.

Little Lake George Ocala NF, 352-625-2520. Est. 1984.
  2,833 acres: wetland and lake.
  Little brother of Florida's largest freshwater lake.
  Near Silver Springs.

Mud Swamp–New River Apalachicola NF, 850-643-2282. Est. 1984.
  8,090 acres: wetland forest.
  The New River supports many threatened reptiles.
  Near Bristol.

National Key Deer National Key Deer NWR, 305-872-2239. Est. 1975.
  2,278 acres: wetland forest.
  Home to the last 300 endangered Key deer.
  Near Big Pine Key.

Passage Key Chassahowitz NWR, 352-563-2088. Est. 1970.
  36 acres: island sandbar.
  The island is closed to the public.
  Near Crystal River.

Pelican Island Merritt Island NWR, 407-861-0667. Est. 1970.
  6 acres: island wetland.
  The first designated wildlife refuge in the United States; island is
     closed to public.
  Near Crystal River.

Saint Marks Saint Marks NWR, 850-925-6121. Est. 1975.
  17,350 acres: wetland and upland forest.
  Home to the manatee and American alligator.
  Near Newport.

GEORGIA

Big Frog (*see* Tennessee).

Blackbeard Island Savannah NWR, 912-652-4415. Est. 1975.
    3,000 acres: island dunes and maritime forest.
    Named for the dread pirate Blackbeard.
    Near Savannah.

Blood Mountain Chattahoochee NF, 706-745-6928. Est. 1991.
    7,800 acres: mountain forest.
    Blood Mountain is a well-known Appalachian Trail landmark.
    Near Dahlonega.

Brasstown Chattahoochee NF, 706-745-6928. Est. 1986.
    12,565 acres: mountain forest.
    4,784-foot Brasstown Bald is the highest point in Georgia.
    Near Blairesville.

Cohutta Chattahoochee NF, 706-695-6737. Est. 1974.
    35,268 acres: mountain forest.
    The largest national forest wilderness east of the Mississippi;
        adjacent to Big Frog Wilderness and home to eastern black bears.
    Near Ellijay.

Cumberland Island Cumberland Island NS, 912-882-4336. Est. 1982.
    8,840 acres: island marsh and maritime forest.
    One of few intact coastal ecosystems that offers excellent hiking and
        backpacking.
    Near Saint Mary's.

Ellicott Rock (*see* North Carolina).

Mark Trail Chattahoochee NF, 706-754-6221. Est. 1991.
   16,400 acres: mountain forest.
   Pine, oak, and maple trees cover the hillsides and support deer and
      woodland birds; also features the AT and several waterfalls.
   Near Helen.

Okefenokee Okefenokee NWR, 912-496-7836. Est. 1974.
   353,981 acres: swamp and peat bog.
   Large and popular wetland recreation area and home to endangered
      wood storks.
   Near Waycross. $

Raven Cliffs Chattahoochee NF, 706-745-6928. Est. 1986.
   9,115 acres: creek and forest.
   Raven Cliff Falls, the AT, and low-elevation mountain habitat.
   Near Helen.

Rich Mountain Chattahoochee NF, 770-632-3031. Est. 1986.
   9,649 acres: mountain forest.
   Healthy populations of deer and other wildlife.
   Near Ellijay.

Southern Nantahala (*see* North Carolina).

Tray Mountain Chattahoochee NF, 706-745-6928. Est. 1986.
   9,702 acres: mountain forest.
   Near the proposed Kelly Ridge Wilderness; riparian habitat along
      Goshen Creek and nearby AT.
   Near Hiawassee.

Wolf Island Savannah NWR, 912-652-4415. Est. 1975.
   5,126 acres: island marsh and beach.
   An important landmark for early 18th century coastal charts.
   Near Savannah.

HAWAII

Haleakala Haleakala NP, 808-572-4400. Est. 1976.
   19,270 acres: island rainforest and volcanic mountain.
   10,023-foot Haleakala Mountain is home to many rare birds.
   Near Makawao. 🥾 $

Hawaii Volcanoes Hawaii Volcanoes NP, 808-985-6000. Est. 1978.
   123,100 acres: volcanic mountain.
   Features Kilauea, the world's most active volcano.
   Near Kona. 🥾 $

IDAHO

Craters of the Moon Craters of the Moon NM, 208-527-3257. Est. 1970.
   43,243 acres: high desert.
   Features a unique volcanic classroom with lava flows, including
       pahoehoe and aa, with cinder cone, spatter cone, and lava tube
       formations.
   Near Arco. 🥾 ⛓ $

Frank Church–River of No Return Salmon-Challis NF, 208-756-2215.
       Est. 1964.
   2.37 million acres: temperate mountain forest.
   Alpine lakes, lush meadows, and steep river canyons, including
       Middle Fork of the Salmon W & SR. Largest wilderness in lower
       48 and home to wolf, wolverine, and lynx.
   Near Salmon. 🥾 🛶 ⌒

Gospel Hump Nez Perce NF, 208-842-2245. Est. 1978.
   206,000 acres: temperate mountain forest.
   Elevations from the Wind River at 1,970-feet to the 8,940-foot
       Buffalo Hump. Habitat for cougar and black bear.
   Near Elk City. 🥾

Hells Canyon (*see* Oregon).

Sawtooth Sawtooth NF, 208-774-3681. Est. 1972.
   217,088 acres: temperate mountain forest.
   Idaho's most famous mountain range; habitat for wolverines and
      reintroduced wolves.
   Near Stanley.

Selway-Bitterroot Nez Perce NF, 208-926-4258. Est. 1964.
   1.09 million acres: mountain forest.
   The rugged Selway Crags and towering Bitterroot Range dominate
      the skyline; includes the Selway W & SR.
   Near Elk City.

ILLINOIS

Bald Knob Shawnee NF, 618-253-7114. Est. 1990.
   5,918 acres: mountain forest.
   North America's largest Christian monument: 111-foot-high, white,
      manmade cross.
   Near Jonesboro.

Bay Creek Shawnee NF, 618-253-7114. Est. 1990.
   2,866 acres: hardwood forest and creek.
   Features Bay Creek W & SR Study Area.
   Near Vienna.

Burden Falls Shawnee NF, 618-253-7114. Est. 1990.
   3,723 acres: hardwood forest and creek.
   Scenic Burden Creek Falls.
   Near Vienna.

Clear Springs Shawnee NF, 618-253-7114. Est. 1990.
    4,730 acres: forested ridges.
    Rough wild slopes and narrow creek bottoms.
    Near Jonesboro.

Crab Orchard Crab Orchard NWR, 618-997-3344. Est. 1976.
    4,050 acres: forest and wetland.
    Nearby 6910-acre Crab Orchard Lake.
    Near Carterville. $

Garden of the Gods Shawnee NF, 618-253-7114. Est. 1990.
    3,293 acres: rocky forest.
    Unusual rock formations with names like "Fat Man's Squeeze" and
        "Tower of Babble."
    Near Elizabethtown.

Lusk Creek Shawnee NF, 618-253-7114. Est. 1990.
    4,796 acres: forest and creeks.
    Scenic views from Indian Kitchen.
    Near Vienna.

Panther Den Shawnee NF, 618-253-7114. Est. 1990.
    940 acres: rocky forest.
    The rock formation known as the Panther Den.
    Near Murphysboro.

INDIANA

Charles C. Dean Hoosier NF, 812-275-5987. Est. 1982.
    12,953 acres: rolling forest.
    Oak-hickory forest supports abundant wildlife, including ruffed
        grouse, wild turkey, and red foxes.
    Near Bedford.

KENTUCKY

Beaver Creek Daniel Boone NF, 606-745-3100. Est. 1975.
    4,791 acres: cliffs, forest, and creeks.
    Healthy populations of white-tailed deer, grouse, and foxes.
    Near Winchester.

Clifty Daniel Boone NF, 606-745-3100. Est. 1985.
    12,646 acres: canyon creeks.
    Unique cliff overhangs of the Red River Gorge area.
    Near Winchester.

LOUISIANA

Breton Southeast Louisiana NWR, 504-646-7555. Est. 1975.
    5,000 acres: tidal forest islands.
    Black mangrove forest on Breton and Chandeleur islands.
    Near Slidell.

Kisatchie Kisatchie NF, 318-473-7160. Est. 1980.
    8,679 acres: dry forest.
    Deep sandy soils, desertlike growing conditions, stunted oaks, and
        flat-topped mesas.
    Near Pineville.

Lacassine Lacassine NWR, 318-774-5923. Est. 1976.
    3,346 acres: wetland.
    Important waterfowl nesting and Louisiana black bear habitat.
    Near Arthur.

MAINE

Caribou–Speckled Mountain White Mountain NF, 207-824-2134. Est. 1990.

12,000 acres: alpine and mountain forest.

Views from 2,877-foot Speckled Mountain and fall colors of mixed hardwood forest.

Near Bethel. 🥾

Moosehorn Moosehorn NWR, 207-454-7161. Est. 1970.

7,392 acres: forest and wetland.

Black bears, moose, and many migratory birds abound.

Near Calais.

MASSACHUSETTS

Monomoy Monomoy NWR, 508-945-0594. Est. 1970.

2,420 acres: coastal beaches and scrub.

Cape Cod offers nesting for fragile populations of piping plovers.

Near Chatham. 🥾

MICHIGAN

Big Island Lake Hiawatha NF, 906-387-3700. Est. 1987.

6,008 acres: forest and lake.

Fragile populations of trout in clear, clean lakes.

Near Munising. 🛶

Delirium Hiawatha NF, 906-635-5311. Est. 1987.

12,000 acres: forest and wetland.

Wild and inaccessible forest swamp habitat.

Near Sault St. Marie.

Horseshoe Bay Hiawatha NF, 906-643-7900. Est. 1987.
   3,949 acres: lakeside beach and forested ridges.
   Lake Huron shore creates habitat for waterfowl and white-tailed deer.
   Near St. Ignace. 🥾

Huron Islands Seney NWR, 906-586-9851. Est. 1970.
   147 acres: islands.
   Lichen-covered rocks, pine forest, and nesting herring gulls; only light
      house open to public.
   Near Seney. 🛶 $

Isle Royale Isle Royale NP, 906-482-0984. Est. 1976.
   132,018 acres: island forest.
   Wild wolves and moose, pristine forest, and remote rugged
      shoreline.
   Near Houghton. 🛶 🥾 🎣 ⌣ $

Mackinac Hiawatha NF, 906-643-7900. Est. 1987.
   12,388 acres: riparian forest.
   Second growth forest and Carp W & SR.
   Near St. Ignace. 🎣 ⌣

McCormick Ottawa NF, 906-852-3501. Est. 1987.
   16,850 acres: forest and wetland.
   The Yellow Dog W & SR and critical habitat for pine martens.
   Near Marquette. 🥾 🎣 ⌣

Michigan Islands Shiawassee NWR, 517-777-5930. Est. 1970.
   12 acres: islands.
   Pismire and Shoes islands support gulls and great blue herons.
   Near Saginaw. 🛶

Nordhouse Dunes Manistee NF, 616-723-2211. Est. 1987.
   3,450 acres: forest and dunes.
   Extensive 3,500- to 4000-year-old lakeshore dune ecosystem, some
      400 feet high.
   Near Manistee. 🥾

Rock River Canyon Hiawatha NF, 906-387-3700. Est. 1987.
　　5,285 acres: forest and canyon.
　　Deep canyon and dense vegetation.
　　Near Marquette.

Round Island Hiawatha NF, 906-643-7900. Est. 1987.
　　378 acres: island.
　　Known for the adjacent Round Island Lighthouse.
　　Near St. Ignace.

Seney Seney NWR, 906-586-9851. Est. 1970.
　　25,150 acres: wetland and forest.
　　Wildlife from otters to osprey and even wolves.
　　Near Seney.

Sturgeon River Gorge Ottawa NF, 906-852-3501. Est. 1987.
　　14,850 acres: forest and canyon.
　　The Sturgeon W & SR offers remote fishing and floating.
　　Near Munising.

Sylvania Ottawa NF, 906-358-4724. Est. 1987.
　　18,327 acres: forest, lakes, and beaches.
　　Expansive virgin forest and habitat for northern pike and walleye.
　　Near Watersmeet. $

MINNESOTA

Agassiz Agassiz NWR, 218-449-4115. Est. 1976.
　　4,000 acres: forest and wetland.
　　Transition area from coniferous forest to prairie pothole region of the
　　　　Red River, supporting 280 species of birds.
　　Near Thief River Falls.

Boundary Waters Canoe Area Superior NF, 218-626-4300. Est. 1964.
   1.09 million acres: forest and wetland.
   Legendary paddling and habitat for wolves, moose, and black bears.
   Near Duluth. 🪶 ⌣ $

Tamarac Tamarac NWR, 218-847-2641. Est. 1976.
   2,180 acres: forest and prairie.
   Resident gray wolf pack.
   Near Detroit Lakes. 👣 ⌣

MISSISSIPPI

Black Creek Desoto NF, 601-928-4422. Est. 1984.
   5,052 acres: wetland.
   Bald cypress and loblolly pine floodplain of Black Creek W & SR.
   Near Wiggins. 👣 🪶 ⌣

Gulf Islands Gulf Islands NS, 228-875-0821. Est. 1978.
   4,637 acres: island wetland and beach.
   Preserves some of the last undisturbed gulf islands.
   Near Gulfport. 🛶 🪶 ⌣

Leaf Desoto NF, 601-928-5291. Est. 1984.
   994 acres: wetland forest.
   Sloughs and floodplains along the Leaf River.
   Near Jackson. 👣 🪶 ⌣

MISSOURI

Bell Mountain Mark Twain NF, 573-438-5427. Est. 1980.
   9,027 acres: mountain forest.
   Scenic views from 1700-foot Bell Mountain.
   Near Potosi.

Devil's Backbone Mark Twain NF, 417-469-3155. Est. 1980.
   6,595 acres: forest, springs, and hills.
   The "backbone" is a rugged ridgeline.
   Near Willow Springs.

Hercules-Glades Mark Twain NF, 417-683-4428. Est. 1976.
   12,315 acres: grassland and forested hills.
   Native tallgrass prairie and oak woodlands.
   Near Ava.

Irish Mark Twain NF, 573-996-2153. Est. 1984.
   16,358 acres: forest, springs, and creeks.
   Home to the endangered Indiana bat and the Eleven Point W & SR.
   Near Doniphan.

Mingo Mingo NWR, 573-222-3589. Est. 1976.
   7,730 acres: forest and wetland.
   Habitat for bald eagles, alligators, snapping turtles, bobolinks,
      dickcissels, and Mississippi kites.
   Near Puxico.

Paddy Creek Mark Twain NF, 573-364-4621. Est. 1983.
   7,059 acres: forest and creek.
   Spectacular views off of razor-edged ridges and bluffs.
   Near Rolla.

Piney Creek Mark Twain NF, 417-847-2144. Est. 1980.
    8,142 acres: forested ridges.
    Tributary to the White River, many limestone glades, and pastureland.
    Near Cassville. ✓

Rockpile Mountain Mark Twain NF, 573-783-7225. Est. 1980.
    4,131 acres: mountain forest.
    Limestone hills, formations, and caves.
    Near Fredericktown. 👣 ◊

MONTANA

Absaroka-Beartooth Gallatin NF, 406-932-5155. Est. 1978.
    944,748 acres (23,283 in Wyoming): alpine and mountain forest.
    10,000-foot plateau lakes and the Greater Yellowstone Ecosystem.
    Near Big Timber. 👣 ✓ ⌐ ◊

Anaconda-Pintler Beaverhead-Deerlodge NF, 406-859-3211. Est. 1964.
    158,656 acres: alpine and mountain forest.
    Features 10,793-foot West Goat Peak and the CDT.
    Near Anaconda. 👣 ✓

Bob Marshall Flathead NF, 406-387-3800. Est. 1964.
    1.01 million acres: mountain forest and creeks.
    The Chinese Wall and South Fork of Flathead W & SR.
    Near Hungry Horse. 👣 ⌐ ✓

Cabinet Mountains Kootenai NF, 406-293-7773. Est. 1964.
    94,272 acres: alpine and mountain forest.
    Small but fragile population of grizzly bears.
    Near Libby. 👣 ✓

Gates of the Mountains Helena NF, 406-449-5490. Est. 1964.
28,562 acres: arid forest and grassland.
The opening of the Rocky Mountains on the Missouri River; name
coined by Lewis & Clark.
Near Helena.

Great Bear Flathead NF, 406-387-3800. Est. 1978.
286,700 acres: mountain forest.
Next to Glacier National Park and part of the Bob Marshall
Wilderness Complex.
Near Hungry Horse.

Lee Metcalf Gallatin NF, 406-646-7369. Est. 1983.
256,297 acres: apine and dry forest.
Named for United States senator and public lands advocate Lee Metcalf;
the blue ribbon Madison River flows through this country.
Near Gallatin Gateway.

Medicine Lake Medicine Lake NWR, 406-789-2305. Est. 1976.
11,366 acres: lake and grassland.
The rolling dunes and prairie grasses of the Sand Hills.
Near Medicine Lake.

Mission Mountains Flathead NF, 406-837-7500. Est. 1975.
73,877 acres: alpine and mountain forest.
Crucial grizzly bear habitat and corridor from the Bob Marshall
Wilderness.
Near Swan Lake.

Rattlesnake Lolo NF, 406-329-3750. Est. 1980.
33,000 acres: alpine and dry mountain forest.
Features 7,960-foot Stuart Peak and critical watershed.
Near Missoula.

Red Rock Lakes Red Rocks Lake NWR, 406-276-3536. Est. 1980.
    32,350 acres: wetland and grassland.
    Established to help save the trumpeter swan.
    Near Dillon.

Scapegoat Lewis and Clark NF, 406-466-5341. Est. 1972.
    239,936 acres: dry mountain forest.
    Southern portion of the Bob Marshall Wilderness Complex features
        the Rocky Mountain Front.
    Near Choteau.

Selway-Bitterroot (*see* Idaho).

UL Bend Charles M. Russell NWR, 406-538-8706. Est. 1976.
    20,819 acres: wetland and grassland.
    Exceptional deer habitat and the Missouri River Breaks W & SR.
    Near Lewistown.

Welcome Creek Lolo NF, 406-329-3814. Est. 1978.
    28,135 acres: dry mountain forest.
    Blue ribbon Rock Creek.
    Near Philipsburg.

NEBRASKA

Fort Niobrara Fort Niobrara NWR, 402-376-3789. Est. 1976.
    4,635 acres: grassland and forest.
    Habitat for elk, buffalo, and Texas longhorns. Also includes the
        Niobrara W & SR.
    Near Valentine.

Soldier Creek Nebraska NF, 308-432-0300. Est. 1986.
    7,794 acres: grassland and dry forest.
    Native grasses and bushes for deer, raptors, and a few coyotes.
    Near Chadron.

NEVADA

Alta Toquima Toiyabe NF, 702-482-6286. Est. 1989.
    38,000 acres: arid mountain forest.
    Crucial habitat for bighorn sheep.
    Near Tonopah.

Arc Dome Toiyabe NF, 702-482-6286. Est. 1989.
    115,020 acres: arid mountain forest.
    Features 11,711-foot Arc Dome and several permanent creeks.
    Near Tonapah.

Boundary Peak Inyo NF, 760-873-2500. Est. 1989.
    10,000 acres: alpine and arid mountain forest.
    13,143-foot Boundary Peak is the highest point in Nevada.
    Near Basalt.

Currant Mountain Humboldt NF, 702-289-3031. Est. 1989.
    36,003 acres: desert and arid mountain forest.
    Features 11,500-foot Currant Mountain and habitat for bighorn
        sheep.
    Near Ely.

East Humboldts Humboldt NF, 702-738-5171. Est. 1989.
    36,900 acres: alpine, arid forest, and desert.
    Healthy populations of mountain lions and mule deer.
    Near Wells.

Grant Range Humboldt NF, 702-289-3031. Est. 1989.
    50,000 acres: arid forest and desert.
    Home to several species of bats and five species of mice.
    Near Sunnyside.

Jarbidge Humboldt NF, 702-738-5171. Est. 1989.
    113,327 acres: alpine and mountain forest.
    Eight peaks over 10,000 feet.
    Near Elko.

Mount Charleston Toiyabe NF, 702-873-8800. Est. 1989.
 43,000 acres: arid mountain forest and desert.
 Features 11,918-foot Mount Charleston.
 Near Las Vegas.

Mount Rose Toiyabe NF, 702-882-2766. Est. 1989.
 28,000 acres: arid mountain forest.
 Lush canyon bottoms to the 10,776-foot summit of Mount Rose.
 Near Reno.

Mount Moriah Humboldt NF, 702-289-3031. Est. 1989.
 76,435 acres: arid mountain forest and grassland.
 Features 12,067-foot Mount Moriah, bristlecone pines, and the Table.
 Near Baker.

Quinn Canyon Humboldt NF, 702-289-3031. Est. 1989.
 27,000 acres: desert canyon and some arid forest.
 Remote canyon adventures.
 Near Elko.

Ruby Mountains Humboldt NF, 702-738-5171. Est. 1989.
 90,000 acres: alpine and mountain forest.
 Features 11,387-foot Ruby Dome and several fragile trout
     populations.
 Near Wells.

Santa Rosa–Paradise Peak Humboldt NF, 702-738-5171. Est. 1989.
 31,000 acres: dry mountain forest and creeks.
 High ridgeline collects enough moisture to support many wildflowers.
 Near Winnemucca.

Table Mountain Toiyabe NF, 702-482-6286. Est. 1989.
 98,000 acres: arid forest and desert.
 A few creeks and canyons support healthy big game populations.
 Near Tonopah.

NEW HAMPSHIRE

Great Gulf White Mountain NF, 603-466-2713. Est. 1964.
   5,552 acres: mountain forest.
   Neighbor to Mount Washington and Pinkham Notch.
   Near Gorham. 🥾 $

Pemigewasset White Mountain NF, 603-536-1310. Est. 1984.
   45,000 acres: mountain forest.
   Section of the AT, waterfalls, and the fabled Bondcliff Knife Edge.
   Near Plymouth. 🥾 $ 🔗

Presidential Range–Dry River White Mountain NF, 603-528-8721.
       Est. 1975.
   27,380 acres: mountain forest.
   Arethusa Falls is one of the tallest waterfalls in New Hampshire.
   Near Bartlett. 🥾 $ 🔗

Sandwich Range White Mountain NF, 603-528-8721. Est. 1984.
   25,000 acres: mountain forest.
   Black bear habitat and 4,015-foot Mount Whiteface.
   Near Plymouth. 🥾 $ 🔗

NEW JERSEY

Brigantine Edwin B. Forsyth NWR, 609-652-1665. Est. 1975.
   6,681 acres: coastal wetland.
   Waterfowl habitat and the last undeveloped barrier beaches along
       the Atlantic Coast.
   Near Oceanville. 🥾

Great Swamp Great Swamp NWR, 609-646-9310. Est. 1968.
  3,660 acres: wetland.
  This important watershed protects habitat for many raptors.
  Near Pleasantville. ✦ ∪

NEW MEXICO

Aldo Leopold Gila NF, 505-388-8201. Est. 1980.
  202,016 acres: arid mountain forest.
  Named for legendary conservationist and wilderness advocate Aldo
    Leopold; includes 10,011-foot Reeds Peak in the rugged Black
    Range.
  Near Silver City. 👣 ◯ ∪

Apache Kid Cibola NF, 505-761-4650. Est. 1980.
  44,626 acres: arid mountain forest.
  Named for the Indian renegade Apache Kid who was wanted dead or
    alive in the 1890s; features dense forest, views, solitude, and
    10,139-foot San Mateo Peak.
  Near Truth of Consequences. 👣

Bandelier Bandelier NM, 505-672-0343. Est. 1976.
  23,267 acres: desert canyons and cliffs.
  Cliff-dwellings of 13th-century Pueblo Indians.
  Near Los Alamos. 👣 $

Bisti Farmington BLM, 505-599-8900. Est. 1984.
  3,946 acres: desert badlands.
  Features pinnacles, hoodoos, arches, and other sandstone formations.
  Near Farmington. 👣

Blue Range Apache NF, 520-339-4384. Est. 1980.
  29,304 acres: arid mountain forest and desert.
  Wolf recovery area includes the Mogollon Rim.
  Near Silver City. 👣

Bosque del Apache Bosque del Apache NWR, 505-835-1828. Est. 1975.
30,287 acres: riverside forest.
The Rio Grande creates habitat for sandhill cranes and Arctic geese.
Near Socorro.

Capitan Mountains Lincoln NF, 505-257-4095. Est. 1980.
35,967 acres: arid mountain forest.
The "birthplace of Smokey Bear."
Near Carrizozo.

Carslbad Caverns Carlsbad Caverns NP, 505-785-2232. Est. 1978.
33,125 acres: caverns and desert.
Nation's deepest limestone cave at -1,597 feet.
Near Carlsbad.

Cebolla El Malpais NCA, 505-285-5406. Est. 1987.
62,800 acres: desert mesas and canyons.
Sheer cliffs offer good nesting habitat for raptors.
Near Grants. $

Chama River Canyon Santa Fe NF, 505-438-7840. Est. 1978.
50,300 acres: desert canyon and river.
Rio Chama W & SR is known for whitewater through a steep-walled
canyon and wonderfully exposed rocks and towers.
Near Espanola. $

Cruces Basin Carson NF, 505-758-8678. Est. 1980.
18,000 acres: arid forest and grassland.
Healthy habitat for deer and other grazing animals.
Near Taos.

De-Na-Zin Farmington BLM, 505-599-8900. Est. 1984.
24,000 acres: desert badlands.
Beautiful rust, gray, red, black, and white mesas.
Near Farmington.

Dome Santa Fe NF, 505-758-7840. Est. 1980.
    5,200 acres: desert canyons and cliffs.
    Cliff-dwellings and colorful rock layers.
    Near Los Alamos.

Gila Gila NF, 505-388-8201. Est. 1964.
    558,065 acres: dry mountain forest.
    The wild area along the southern Continental Divide became the
        first wilderness designated by Congress.
    Near Silver City.

Latir Peak Carson NF, 505-586-0520. Est. 1980.
    20,000 acres: alpine and mountain forest.
    Several creeks and nearby lakes beside 12,000-foot peaks.
    Near Costilla.

Manzano Mountain Cibola NF, 505-761-4650. Est. 1978.
    37,195 acres: arid mountain forest.
    10,098-foot Manzano Peak is the highest peak in the range.
    Near Belen.

Pecos Santa Fe NF, 505-438-7840. Est. 1964.
    201,073 acres: alpine and mountain forest.
    Features 13,102-foot Truchas Peak and the Pecos W & SR.
    Near Santa Fe.

Salt Creek Bitter Lake NWR, 505-622-6755. Est. 1970.
    9,621 acres: wetland and brushland.
    Only known nesting area in New Mexico for the interior least tern.
    Near Roswell.

Sandia Mountain Cibola NF, 505-761-4650. Est. 1978.
    38,357 acres: arid mountain forest and desert.
    Unique rock outcrops like the "Thumb."
    Near Albuquerque.

San Pedro Parks Santa Fe NF, 505-438-7840. Est. 1964.
    41,132 acres: alpine and mountain forest.
    10,000-foot plateau, big flat meadows, and meandering creeks.
    Near Cuba.

West Malpais El Malpais NCA, 505-285-5406. Est. 1987.
    39,700 acres: arid forest and desert.
    Supports populations of elk, deer, antelope, and mountain lions.
    Near Grants.

Wheeler Peak Carson NF, 505-586-0520. Est. 1964.
    19,663 acres: alpine.
    Highest point in New Mexico at 13,161 feet.
    Near Taos.

White Mountain Lincoln NF, 505-257-4095. Est. 1964.
    48,885 acres: arid forest ridges.
    Habitat for large mammals such as black bears and elk.
    Near Carrizozo.

Withington Cibola NF, 505-761-4650. Est. 1980.
    19,000 acres: arid mountain forest.
    Features solitude, true wilderness, waterfalls, and cool canyons.
    Near Magdalena.

NEW YORK

Fire Island Fire Island NS, 516-289-4810. Est. 1980.
  5,160 acres: coastal wetland and beach.
  Over 7,000 schoolchildren visit the shore annually.
  Near Long Island.

NORTH CAROLINA

Birkhead Mountains Uwharrie NF, 910-576-6391. Est. 1984.
  5,160 acres: mountain forest.
  Possibly the oldest mountains in North America.
  Near Troy.

Catfish Lake South Croatan NF, 919-638-5628. Est. 1984.
  8,530 acres: wetland.
  Shallow lake surrounded by several feeder creeks.
  Near New Bern.

Ellicott Rock Nantahala NF, 704-526-3765. Est. 1975.
  8,274 acres (2,859 in South Carolina and 2,021 in Georgia):
      riverside forest.
  Features the popular Chattooga W & SR.
  Near Highlands.

Joyce Kilmer–Slickrock Nantahala NF, 704-479-6431. Est. 19.
  17,394 acres (3,832 in Tennessee): mountain forest.
  Statton Bald, excellent hiking, and renowned virgin forest.
  Near Robbinsville.

Linville Gorge Pisgah NF, 704-652-2144. Est. 1964.
  12,002 acres: riverside forest and rock.
  The "Grand Canyon" of North Carolina.
  Near Nebo. $

Middle Prong Pisgah NF, 704-877-3350. Est. 1984.
  7,460 acres: forest and creeks.
  Several waterfalls and cool groves.
  Near Brevard.

Pocosin Pocosin Lakes NWR, 919-797-4431. Est. 1984.
  11,709 acres: forest and wetland.
  Habitat for the endangered red-cockaded woodpecker.
  Near Creswell.

Pond Pine Croatan NF, 919-638-5628. Est. 1984.
  1,685 acres: forest and wetland.
  Pond Pine, known as "pocosin pine," is a swamp-dwelling tree.
  Near New Bern.

Sheep Ridge Croatan NF, 919-638-5628. Est. 1984.
  9,297 acres: forested hills.
  Gentle mountain forest provides habitat for deer and other wildlife.
  Near New Bern.

Shining Rock Pisgah NF, 704-877-3350. Est. 1964.
  18,483 acres: mountain forest.
  Named after its distinctive white quartz outcrop.
  Near Sam Knob.

Southern Nantahala Nantahala NF, 704-524-6441. Est. 1984.
  23,714 acres (11,770 in Georgia): mountain forest.
  Features 5,499-foot Standing Indian in the Blue Ridge.
  Near Franklin.

Swanquarter Mattamuskeet NWR, 919-926-4021. Est. 1976.
  8,785 acres: coastal wetland and salt marsh.
  Estuary habitat for canvasbacks, ducks, and osprey.
  Near Swanquarter.

NORTH DAKOTA

Chase Lake Chase Lake NWR, 701-752-4218. Est. 1975.
    4,155 acres: wetland and grassland.
    Wetland "duck factory" established to protect the native white pelican.
    Near Woodsworth. ✓

Lostwood Lostwood NWR, 701-848-2722. Est. 1975.
    5,577 acres: wetland and grassland.
    Important waterfall habitat in the "Prairie Pothole" region of North
        Dakota.
    Near Stanley. ✓

Theodore Roosevelt Theodore Roosevelt NP, 701-623-4466. Est. 1978.
    29,920 acres: prairie badlands.
    The Little Missouri River and habitat for remnant populations of
        bison.
    Near Medora. 🥾 ⚒ $

OHIO

West Sister Island West Sister Island NWR, 800-344-9453. Est. 1975.
    77 acres: island forest.
    The Great Lakes' largest heron and egret rookery. Closed to public
        use.
    Near Port Clinton. 🛶

OKLAHOMA

Black Fork (*see* Arkansas).

Upper Kiamichi Ouachita NF, 501-321-5202. Est. 1988.
   10,819 acres: deciduous mountain forest.
   Rugged slopes along Rich Mountain.
   Near Big Cedar.

Wichita Mountains Wichita Mountains NWR, 580-429-3221.
      Est. 1970.
   8,570 acres: mountain forest.
   Second oldest managed wildlife refuge in United States; home to
      bison and elk.
   Near Indiahoma.

OREGON

Badger Creek Mount Hood NF, 541-467-2291. Est. 1984.
   24,000 acres: mountain forest.
   Badger Lake and the headwaters of Badger Creek.
   Near Hood River. $

Black Canyon Ochoco NF, 541-477-3713. Est. 1984.
   13,400 acres: forest and canyons.
   Habitat for black bear, deer, cougar, and elk.
   Near Paulina.

Boulder Creek Umpqua NF, 541-498-2531. Est. 1984.
   19,100 acres: dry forest.
   Unique volcanic rock formations like Umpqua Rocks.
   Near Diamond Lake.

Bridge Creek Ochoco NF, 541-416-6645. Est. 1984.
   5,400 acres: dry mountain forest.
   Barren plateaus called scab flats.
   Near Prineville.

Bull of the Woods Mount Hood NF, 503-630-6861. Est. 1984.
   34,900 acres: mountain forest.
   Steep, rugged headwaters of Little North Santiam River.
   Near Estacada. 👞 〰 $

Columbia (*see* Mark O. Hatfield).

Cummins Creek Siuslaw NF, 541-563-3211. Est. 1984.
   9,173 acres: dense forest.
   Little-visited coastal wilderness.
   Near Waldport. 👞

Diamond Peak Deschutes NF, 541-433-2234. Est. 1964.
   54,185 acres: alpine and mountain forest.
   Features 8,744-foot Diamond Peak in the Cascade Range and a
      section of the PCT.
   Near Crescent Lake. 👞 〰 ◊ $

Drift Creek Siuslaw NF, 541-563-3211. Est. 1984.
   5,798 acres: coastal forest.
   Important habitat for migratory salmon and steelhead.
   Near Waldport. 🐟 〰

Eagle Cap Wallowa NF, 541-426-4978. Est. 1964.
   360,275 acres: dry mountain forest.
   High peaks, lakes, and vast adventureland.
   Near Pendleton. 👞 〰 ◊

Gearhart Mountain Fremont NF, 541-353-2427. Est. 1964.
   22,809 acres: arid mountain forest.
   Features 8,364-foot Gearhart Mountain.
   Near Bly. 👞

Grassy Knob Siskiyou NF, 541-439-3011. Est. 1984.
  17,200 acres: dense coastal forest.
  Created to protect the anadramous fishery of Dry Creek.
  Near Powers.

Hells Canyon Hells Canyon NRA, 541-426-4978. Est. 1975.
  215,233 acres (84,100 in Idaho): dry canyon.
  Undammed section of the Snake W & SR; wilderness also in Idaho
    and Washington.
  Near Enterprise. $

Kalmiopsis Siskiyou NF, 541-469-2196. Est. 1964.
  179,700 acres: mountain forest.
  The Chetco, Illinois, and North Fork Smith W & SRs.
  Near Brookings. $

Mark O. Hatfield Mount Hood NF, 541-352-6002. Est. 1984.
  39,000 acres: gorge forest and creeks.
  Formerly the Columbia Wilderness. Features upper reaches and
    waterfalls of Eagle Creek.
  Near Cascade Locks.

Menagerie Willamette NF, 541-367-5168. Est. 1984.
  4,800 acres: forest.
  The Menagerie is a series of rock pinnacles including Rooster Rock.
  Near Sweet Home. $

Middle Santiam Willamette NF, 541-367-5168. Est. 1984.
  7,500 acres: peaks and forested benches.
  Important river habitat for native trout.
  Near Sweet Home. $

Mill Creek Ochoco NF, 541-416-6500. Est. 1984.
    17,400 acres: alpine meadows and dry forest.
    Towering pinnacles and deep canyon.
    Near Prineville.

Monument Rock Malheur NF, 541-820-3311. Est. 1984.
    19,650 acres: dry mountain forest.
    Habitat for seven species of birds including the creek-loving American
        dipper.
    Near Unity. $

Mountain Lakes Winema NF, 541-885-3400. Est. 1964.
    23,071 acres: mountain forest.
    Volcanic-formed lake and peaks in the Cascades.
    Near Klammath Falls.

Mount Hood Mount Hood NF, 503-622-7674. Est. 1964.
    47,160 acres: alpine and mountain forest.
    11,239-foot Mount Hood visible from Portland on a clear day.
    Near Government Camp. $

Mount Jefferson Willamette NF, 503-854-3366. Est. 1968.
    107,008 acres: alpine and mountain forest.
    Features 10,497-foot Mount Jefferson and 7,841-foot Three Finger
        Jack.
    Near Mill City. $

Mount Thielsen Winema NF, 541-365-7001. Est. 1984.
    54,267 acres: arid mountain forest.
    Features 9,182-foot Mount Thielsen.
    Near Chemult.

Mount Washington Willamette NF, 541-822-3381. Est. 1964.
    52,738 acres: alpine and mountain forest.
    Features 7,794-foot Mount Washington, Belknap Crater, and the PCT.
    Near Sisters. $

North Fork John Day Umatilla NF, 541-427-3231. Est. 1984.
121,352 acres: dry rolling benchlands.
The North Fork of the John Day W & SR; fish habitat.
Near Ukiah.

North Fork Umatilla Umatilla NF, 509-522-6290. Est. 1984.
20,435 acres: arid forest.
Created to protect the pure water of the North Fork of the Umatilla
River.
Near Pendleton.

Oregon Islands Oregon Coast NWR, 541-757-7236. Est. 1970.
480 acres: coastal islands.
Offshore habitat for sea lions and other wildlife.
Near Port Orford.

Red Buttes (*see* California).

Rock Creek Siuslaw NF, 541-563-3211. Est. 1984.
7,486 acres: coastal temperate rainforest.
Ideal wet and mild habitat for hemlock and cedar forest.
Near Waldport.

Rogue–Umpqua Divide Umpqua NF, 541-825-3201. Est. 1984.
33,200 acres: mountain forest.
Important watershed protection for two famous rivers.
Near Tiller.

Salmon-Huckleberry Mount Hood NF, 503-622-7674. Est. 1984.
44,600 acres: mountain forest.
Important Portland recreation area and home to deer, elk, and black
bears.
Near ZigZag.

Sky Lakes Winema NF, 541-885-3400. Est. 1984.
  116,300 acres: mountain forest.
  Near Crater Lake; features the Middle Fork of the Rogue W & SR.
  Near Diamond Lake.

Strawberry Mountain Malheur NF, 541-820-3311. Est. 1964.
  69,350 acres: alpine and dry mountain forest.
  Features 9,038-foot Strawberry Peak near the John Day River.
  Near Prairie City.

Three Arch Rocks Oregon Coast NWR, 541-867-4550. Est. 1970.
  14 acres: rocky islands.
  Important habitat for marine birds.
  Near Tillamook.

Three Sisters Willamette NF, 541-822-3381. Est. 1964.
  286,708 acres: alpine and mountain forest.
  North, Middle, and South sisters are all above 10,000 feet.
  Near Bend. $

Waldo Lake Willamette NF, 541-782-2283. Est. 1984.
  39,200 acres: mountain forest.
  In the High Cascades; features Waldo Lake, one of the purest in the
    world.
  Near Oakridge. $

Wenaha-Tucannon (*see* Washington).

Wild Rogue Siskiyou NF, 541-247-3600. Est. 1978.
  36,500 acres: riverside forest.
  Created to protect the Rogue W & SR.
  Near Gold Beach. $

PENNSYLVANIA

Allegheny Islands Allegheny NF, 814-723-5150. Est. 1984.
368 acres: river islands.
Crucial waterfowl habitat along the Allegheny W & SR.
Near Tionesta.

Hickory Creek Allegheny NF, 814-723-5150. Est. 1984.
8,570 acres: forest and creeks.
Habitat for pileated woodpeckers and barred owls.
Near Warren.

SOUTH CAROLINA

Cape Romain Cape Romain NWR, 843-928-3368. Est. 1979.
29,000 acres: coastal beach and wetland.
Critical nesting habitat for loggerhead turtles.
Near Mount Pleasant.

Congaree Swamp Congaree Swamp NM, 803-776-4396. Est. 1988.
15,010 acres: wetland forest.
Largest expanse of floodplain forest in America.
Near Hopkins. $

Ellicott Rock (*see* North Carolina).

Hell Hole Bay Francis Marion NF, 803-336-3248. Est. 1980.
2,125 acres: wetland.
Named for burning sodfires that plague the area.
Near Moncks Corner.

Little Wambaw Swamp Francis Marion NF, 803-336-3248. Est. 1980.
5,047 acres: wetland.
Swamp offers habitat for many birds and amphibians.
Near McClellanville.

Wambaw Creek Francis Marion NF, 803-336-3248. Est. 1980.
   1,825 acres: wetland forest.
   Old-growth cypress and habitat for many reptiles.
   Near McClellanville. 🦅 〰️

Wambaw Swamp Francis Marion NF, 803-336-3457. Est. 1980.
   4,815 acres: wetland forest.
   Habitat for copperheads and timber rattlesnakes.
   Near McClellanville. 🦅 〰️

SOUTH DAKOTA

Badlands Badlands NP, 605-433-5361. Est. 1976.
   9,826 acres: dry wash and grassland.
   Eroded layers of sediment create spires, canyons, and ridges.
   Near Interior. 👢 $

Black Elk Black Hills NF, 605-673-4853. Est. 1980.
   9,826 acres: arid forest hills.
   Named for famed Sioux holy man Black Elk.
   Near Rapid City. 👢

TENNESSEE

Bald River Gorge Cherokee NF, 423-476-9700. Est. 1984.
   3,721 acres: mountain forest and canyon.
   Majestic Bald River Falls and colorful rhododendron blooms.
   Near Tellico Plains. 👢 〰️

Big Frog Cherokee NF, 423-338-5201. Est. 1984.
   7,993 acres: mountain forest.
   Features 4,224-foot Big Frog Mountain and nearby Ocoee River.
   Near Cleveland. 👢 🦅 〰️

Big Laurel Branch Cherokee NF, 619-476-9700. Est. 1986.
6,251 acres: mountain forest.
Colorful laurel blooms and views of Watauga Lake.
Near Cleveland.

Citico Creek Cherokee NF, 423-476-9700. Est. 1984.
16,226 acres: mountain forest.
Features Rattlesnake Rock.
Near Cleveland.

Cohutta (*see* Georgia).

Gee Creek Cherokee NF, 619-476-9700. Est. 1975.
2,493 acres: mountain forest.
Habitat for owls and bluebirds.
Near Cleveland.

Joyce Kilmer–Slickrock (*see* North Carolina).

Little Frog Mountain Cherokee NF, 423-476-9700. Est. 1986.
4,666 acres: mountain forest.
The nearby Ocoee River served as the Olympic venue for whitewater
events.
Near Cleveland.

Pond Mountain Cherokee NF, 423-476-9700. Est. 1986.
6,665 acres: mountain forest.
Wild and rugged Laurel Fork Gorge.
Near Hampton.

Sampson Mountain Cherokee NF, 423-476-9700. Est. 1986.
7,992 acres: mountain forest.
Hemlock and pine forest on Sampson Mountain.
Near Erwin.

Unaka Mountain Cherokee NF, 423-476-9700. Est. 1986.
    4,496 acres: mountain forest.
    5,180-foot Unaka Mountain offers views of the Black Mountains.
    Near Cleveland.

TEXAS

Big Slough Davy Crockett NF, 409-655-2299. Est. 1984.
    3,455 acres: wetland forest.
    Principally a hardwood bottom with oaks and willows.
    Near Kennard.

Guadalupe Mountains Guadalupe Mountains NP, 915-828-3251.
        Est. 1978.
    46,850 acres: desert mountains.
    The world's most significant Permian limestone fossil reef.
    Near El Paso. $

Indian Mounds Sabine NF, 409-787-3870. Est. 1984.
    12,369 acres: hill forest.
    Unique Indian Mound formations. Pine forest is threatened by the
        Southern pine beetle.
    Near Hemphill.

Little Lake Creek Sam Houston NF, 409-344-6205. Est. 1984.
    3,855 acres: forest and wetland.
    Forest recoverving from pine beetle infestation.
    Near New Waverly.

Turkey Hill Angelina NF, 409-639-8620. Est. 1984.
    5,473 acres: hill forest.
    Reintroduced turkeys makes this a popular area for hunters.
    Near Lufkin.

Upland Island Angelina NF, 409-639-8620. Est. 1984.
   13,331 acres: forest.
   Habitat for red crossbills.
   Near Zavalla.

UTAH

Ashdown Gorge Dixie NF, 801-865-3700. Est. 1984.
   7,000 acres: arid forest and desert.
   Features 2,000-year-old bristlecone pines and Wasatch limestone cliffs.
   Near Cedar City. 👟

Beaver Dam Mountains (*see* Arizona).

Box–Death Hollow Grand Staircase–Escalante NM, 801-826-5499.
      Est. 1984.
   25,814 acres: desert canyons.
   Thirty-mile Death Hollow Canyon.
   Near Loa. 👟

Dark Canyon Manti-La Sal NF, 801-587-2041. Est. 1984.
   45,000 acres: arid forest and desert canyon.
   Features 2,000-foot-high sandstone canyon walls.
   Near Moab. 👟

Deseret Peak Wasatch-Cache NF, 801-943-1794. Est. 1984.
   25,500 acres: arid mountain forest and shrubland.
   Features 11,031-foot Deseret Peak; popular Salt Lake destination.
   Near Grantsville. 👟

High Uintas Ashley NF, 801-783-4338. Est. 1984.
   456,705 acres: alpine and dry mountain forest.
   Dozen peaks over 13,000 feet.
   Near Mountain Home. 👟 〰️ 🧗

Lone Peak Uinta NF, 801-943-1794. Est. 1978.
    30,088 acres: alpine and dry forest.
    Features 11,253-foot Lone Peak and others.
    Near Alpine.

Mount Naomi Wasatch-Cache NF, 801-755-3620. Est. 1984.
    44,350 acres: dry mountain forest.
    9,979-foot Naomi Peak is the highest point in the Bear River
        Mountains.
    Near Logan.

Mount Nebo Uinta NF, 801-342-5260. Est. 1984.
    28,000 acres: mountain brushland.
    Named for the original Mount Nebo in Palestine.
    Near Spanish Fork.

Mount Olympus Wasatch-Cache NF, 801-943-1794. Est. 1984.
    16,000 acres: arid mountain forest.
    Wasatch Front landmark, 9,026-foot Mount Olympus.
    Near Salt Lake City.

Mount Timpanogos Uinta NF, 801-785-3563. Est. 1984.
    10,750 acres: arid mountain forest.
    One of the most popular climbs in the Wasatch Range.
    Near Salt Lake City.

Paria Canyon–Vermilion Cliffs (*see* Arizona).

Pine Valley Mountain Dixie NF, 801-865-3700. Est. 1984.
    50,000 acres: arid forest and scrubland.
    Virgin stands of limber pine.
    Near New Harmony.

Twin Peaks Wasatch-Cache NF, 801-943-1794. Est. 1984.
   11,463 acres: arid mountain forest.
   These 11,000-foot peaks are popular hiking destinations.
   Near Salt Lake City.

Wellsville Mountain Wasatch-Cache NF, 801-755-3620. Est. 1984.
   23,850 acres: arid mountain forest.
   Prime example of ecosystem recovery from early over-grazing.
   Near Brigham City.

VERMONT

Big Branch Green Mountain NF, 802-362-2307. Est. 1984.
   6,720 acres: mountain forest.
   Roaring brooks, pristine lakes, and scenic mountainsides await.
   Near Manchester.

Breadloaf Green Mountain NF, 802-388-4362. Est. 1984.
   21,480 acres: mountain forest.
   Features the Long Trail and 3,835-foot Breadloaf Mountain.
   Near Middlebury.

Bristol Cliffs Green Mountain NF, 802-388-4362. Est. 1975.
   3,738 acres: rock and mountain forest.
   Popular rock climbing area.
   Near Middlebury.

George D. Aiken Green Mountain NF, 802-362-2307. Est. 1984.
   5,060 acres: mountain forest.
   Excellent foliage and fall colors in this New England forest.
   Near Manchester.

Lye Brook Green Mountain NF, 802-362-2307. Est. 1975.
   15,680 acres: plateau forest and wetland.
   Features views from Prospect Rock and Stratton Mountain, above
      famed Stratton Pond and Lyle Brook; also a section of the AT.
   Near Manchester.

Peru Peak Green Mountain NF, 802-362-2307. Est. 1984.
   6,920 acres: mountain forest.
   Spectacular view off this prominent 3,429-foot-high peak.
   Near Manchester.

VIRGINIA

Barbours Creek Jefferson NF, 540-864-5195. Est. 1988.
   5,382 acres: mountain forest.
   Lush hemlock and pine forest along Barbours Creek.
   Near New Castle.

Beartown Jefferson NF, 540-552-4641. Est. 1984.
   5,609 acres: mountain forest.
   Virginia's most remote wild area accessible via the AT.
   Near Blacksburg.

James River Face Jefferson NF, 540-291-2189. Est. 1975.
   8,886 acres: mountain forest and canyon.
   Often grouped with Thunder Ridge and includes the wild James River
      Gorge.
   Near Glenwood.

Kimberling Creek Jefferson NF, 540-552-4641. Est. 1984.
   5,542 acres: mountain forest.
   Habitat for deer, turkey, and native trout.
   Near Blacksburg.

Lewis Fork Mount Rogers NRA, 540-783-5196. Est. 1984.
   5,618 acres: mountain forest.
   Features 5,792-foot Mount Rogers, highest point in Virginia.
   Near Marion.

Little Dry Run Mount Rogers NRA, 540-783-5196. Est. 1984.
   2,858 acres: mountain forest.
   Habitat for native trout.
   Near Marion.

Little Wilson Creek Mount Rogers NRA, 540-783-5196. Est. 1984.
   3,613 acres: mountain forest.
   Features steep, rocky slopes and several springs.
   Near Marion.

Mountain Lake Jefferson NF, 540-552-4641. Est. 1984.
   11,113 acres (2,721 in West Virginia): mountain forest and wetland.
   One of few truly natural lakes in the area.
   Near Blacksburg.

Peters Mountain Jefferson NF, 540-552-4641. Est. 1984.
   3,328 acres: mountain forest.
   3,956-foot Peters Mountain and sandstone outcrops.
   Near Blacksburg.

Ramsey's Draft George Washington NF, 540-885-8028. Est. 1984.
   6,518 acres: dry ridge and forest.
   Ancient hemlock forest.
   Near Staunton.

Rich Hole George Washington NF, 540-962-2214. Est. 1988.
   6,450 acres: mountain forest.
   Named for rich soils at the head of small drainages.
   Near Covington.

Rough Mountain George Washington NF, 540-839-2521. Est. 1988.
    9,300 acres: mountain forest.
    Upland hardwoods and southern white pine forest.
    Near Hot Springs.

Saint Mary's George Washington NF, 540-291-2189. Est. 1984.
    9,835 acres: cool forest.
    Quartzite rock and scenic waterfalls.
    Near Covington.

Shenandoah Shenandoah NP, 540-999-3500. Est. 1976.
    79,579 acres: mountain forest.
    Home of the famous Blue Ridge Mountains and Parkway.
    Near Luray. $

Shawyers Run Jefferson NF, 540-864-5195. Est. 1988.
    3,467 acres: mountain forest.
    Features 3,800-foot Hanging Rock.
    Near New Castle.

Thunder Ridge Jefferson NF, 540-291-2189. Est. 1984.
    2,344 acres: mountain forest.
    Features 4,200-foot Apple Orchard Mountains.
    Near Natural Bridge Station.

WASHINGTON

Alpine Lakes Mount Baker–Snoqualmie NF, 425-775-9702. Est. 1976.
    364,229 acres: alpine and mountain forest.
    Washington's most popular wilderness features many high lakes and
        trails.
    Near Stevens Pass. $

Boulder River Mount Baker–Snoqualmie NF, 425-775-9702. Est. 1984.
  48,674 acres: mountain forest.
  Ice-clad summits of Three-Fingers and Whitehorse Mountain, and
    the North Fork of the "Stilly."
  Near Darrington.

Buckhorn Olympic NF, 360-765-2200. Est. 1984.
  44,474 acres: temperate rainforest.
  Mountains and valleys of old-growth trees are threatened by a
    mining patent.
  Near Quilcene. $

Clearwater Mount Baker–Snoqualmie NF, 425-775-9702. Est. 1984.
  14,374 acres: alpine and mountain forest.
  Spectacular views of Mount Rainier.
  Near Tacoma. $

Colonel Bob Olympic NF, 360-288-2525. Est. 1984.
  11,961 acres: alpine and temperate rainforest.
  Rugged peaks and old-growth stands of Sitka spruce and western
    redcedar.
  Near Quinault.

Glacier Peak Mount Baker–Snoqualmie NF, 425-775-9702. Est. 1964.
  572,738 acres: alpine and mountain forest.
  Features 10,541-foot Glacier Peak.
  Near Stevens Pass. $

Glacier View Gifford Pinchot NF, 360-891-5000. Est. 1984.
  3,123 acres: alpine and mountain forest.
  Features the Goat Lake Trail and views of Mount Rainier glaciers.
  Near Paradise. $

Goat Rocks Gifford Pinchot NF, 360-891-5000. Est. 1964.
> 108,439 acres: mountain forest.
> Excellent view of Johnson Peak and Packwood Lake.
> Near Packwood.

Henry M. Jackson Mount Baker–Snoqualmie NF, 425-775-9702.
> Est. 1984.
> 100,867 acres: alpine and mountain forest.
> Cady Creek Ridge and the PCT.
> Near Skykomish.

Indian Heaven Gifford Pinchot NF, 360-891-5000. Est. 1984.
> 20,960 acres: mountain forest.
> Popular area on the Cascade divide and includes a section of the
> PCT.
> Near Trout Lake. $

Juniper Dunes Spokane BLM, 509-536-1200. Est. 1984.
> 6,900 acres: arid forest and dunes.
> Difficult access and little use.
> Near Spokane.

Lake Chelan–Sawtooth Okanogan NF, 509-997-2131. Est. 1984.
> 151,522 acres: alpine and mountain forest.
> North Cascades feature many peaks over 8,000 feet.
> Near Stehekin.

Mount Adams Gifford Pinchot NF, 360-891-5000. Est. 1964.
> 56,681 acres: alpine and mountain forest.
> Features 12,307-foot Mount Adams.
> Near Trout Lake. $

Mount Baker Mount Baker–Snoqualmie NF, 425-775-9702. Est. 1984.
> 117,848 acres: alpine and mountain forest.
> 10,778-foot Mount Baker is a popular destination for mountaineers.
> Near Bellingham. $

Mount Rainier Mount Rainier NP, 360-569-2211. Est. 1988.
228,488 acres: alpine and mountain forest.
14,410-foot Mount Rainier is a world-class climb and the highest
point in Washington.
Near Tacoma. $

Mount Skokomish Olympic NF, 360-877-5254. Est. 1984.
13,015 acres: alpine and mountain forest.
Barren ridges and steep rock outcrops.
Near Hoodsport.

Noisy-Diobsud Mount Baker–Snoqualmie NF, 425-775-9702. Est. 1984.
14,133 acres: alpine and mountain forest.
On the steep slopes next to North Cascades National Park.
Near Rockport.

Norse Peak Mount Baker–Snoqualmie NF, 425-775-9702. Est. 1984.
52,180 acres: alpine and mountain forest.
High volcanic peaks and lakes straddle the Cascades.
Near Mountlake Terrace.

Olympic Olympic NP, 360-452-0330. Est. 1988.
876,669 acres: alpine and temperate rainforest.
Features old-growth cedar and hemlock in the Hoh Rainforest.
Near Port Angeles. $

Pasayten Okanogan NF, 509-997-2131. Est. 1968.
530,031 acres: alpine and mountain forest.
Virgin stands of temperate old-growth fir and spruce.
Near Mazama.

Salmo-Priest Colville NF, 509-684-7000. Est. 1984.
41,335 acres: mountain forest.
Important grizzly bear recovery habitat.
Near Kettle Falls.

San Juan Islands Nisqually NWR, 360-753-9467. Est. 1976.
   353 acres: island temperate rainforest.
   Puget Sound habitat for everything from sea birds to killer whales.
     Most of refuge is closed to public.
   Near Bellingham.

Stephen Mather North Cascades NP, 360-856-5700. Est. 1988.
   634,614 acres: alpine and mountain forest.
   High cascade peaks, glaciers, and grizzly bear habitat.
   Near Near Winthrop. $

Tatoosh Gifford Pinchot NF, 360-891-5000. Est. 1984.
   15,750 acres: alpine and mountain forest.
   Ridges, dense forest, and creeks near Mount Rainier.
   Near Packwood.

The Brothers Olympic NF, 360-877-5254. Est. 1984.
   16,682 acres: alpine and mountain forest.
   6,866-foot The Brothers and heavily forested steep ridges.
   Near Hoodsport.

Trapper Creek Gifford Pinchot NF, 360-891-5000. Est. 1984.
   5,970 acres: forest and creek.
   Headwaters of the Wind River and habitat for salmon.
   Near Trout Lake. $

Washington Islands Nisqually NWR, 360-753-9467. Est. 1970.
   486 acres: temperate island rainforest.
   Puget Sound habitat for whales and sea birds.
   Near Olympia.

Wenaha-Tucannon Umatilla NF, 541-278-3716. Est. 1978.
   177,465 acres (66,417 in Oregon): dry forested ridge.
   Includes the Wenaha W & SR and 6,401-foot Oregon Butte.
   Near Walla Walla.

William O. Douglas Wenatchee NF, 509-653-2205. Est. 1984.
  168,157 acres: mountain forest.
  Many views, lakes, and a section of the PCT.
  Near Naches.

Wonder Mountain Olympic NF, 360-877-5254. Est. 1984.
  2,349 acres: alpine and mountain forest.
  Rugged pinnacles top some ridges.
  Near Hoodsport.

WEST VIRGINIA

Cranberry Monongahela NF, 304-636-1800. Est. 1983.
  35,864 acres: forest, wetland, and meadows.
  Highlights include Cranberry Glade—750 acres bog of spongy
    floating peat, and trout fishing on the Cranberry River.
  Near Elkins.

Dolly Sods Monongahela NF, 304-636-1800. Est. 1975.
  10,215 acres: wetland plains.
  Bogs, beaver ponds, and scenic views from the Allegheny Plateau.
  Near Elkins.

Laurel Fork North Monongahela NF, 304-636-1800. Est. 1983.
  6,055 acres: mountain forest and wetland.
  Headwaters of the Cheat River.
  Near Elkins.

Laurel Fork South Monongahela NF, 304-636-1800. Est. 1983.
  5,997 acres: mountain forest and wetlands.
  Important watershed for Cheat River.
  Near Elkins.

Mountain Lake (*see* Virginia).

Otter Creek Monongahela NF, 304-636-1800. Est. 1974.
   20,000 acres: mountain forest.
   Second-growth timber; Otter Creek and Shavers Lick Run.
   Near Petersburg.

WISCONSIN

Blackjack Springs Nicolet NF, 715-528-4464. Est. 1978.
   5,886 acres: forest and wetland.
   Cool springs and birch groves.
   Near Laona.

Headwaters Nicolet NF, 715-528-4464. Est. 1984.
   20,104 acres: forest and wetland.
   Old-growth forest and waterfowl habitat.
   Near Laona.

Porcupine Lake Chequamegon NF, 715-762-2461. Est. 1984.
   4,446 acres: forest and wetland.
   Short secluded hike to this beautiful lake.
   Near Medford.

Rainbow Lake Chequamegon NF, 715-762-2461. Est. 1975.
   6,583 acres: forest and wetland.
   Includes section of the NCT.
   Near Cable.

Whisker Lake Nicolet NF, 715-528-4464. Est. 1978.
   7,428 acres: forest and wetlands.
   Old, second-growth pine forest and black bear habitat.
   Near Florence.

Wisconsin Islands Horicon NWR, 920-387-2658. Est. 1970.
    29 acres: island forest.
    Nation's smallest wilderness area.
    Near Maysville.

WYOMING

Absaroka-Beartooth (*see* Montana).

Bridger Bridger-Teton NF, 307-739-5500. Est. 1964.
    428,087 acres: alpine and mountain forest.
    Part of the Wind River Range with craggy peaks and secluded lakes.
    Near Dubois.

Cloud Peak Bighorn NF, 307-672-0751. Est. 1984.
    189,039 acres: alpine and dry mountain forest.
    Island range has many lakes and peaks to explore.
    Near Sheridan.

Encampment River Medicine Bow NF, 307-745-2300. Est. 1984.
    10,124 acres: dry forest and creek.
    Headwaters of the blue ribbon Platte River.
    Near Riverside.

Fitzpatrick Shoshone NF, 307-332-5460. Est. 1976.
    198,525 acres: alpine and mountain forest.
    High alpine hiking and fishing.
    Near Lander.

Gros Ventre Bridger-Teton NF, 307-739-5500. Est. 1984.
    287,000 acres: alpine and mountain forest.
    Features 10,775-foot Pinnacle Peak.
    Near Jackson.

Huston Park Medicine Bow NF, 307-745-2300. Est. 1984.
    30,726 acres: alpine and dry forest.
    A section of the CDT on its way to Colorado.
    Near Riverside.

Jedediah Smith Targhee NF, 208-624-3151. Est. 1984.
    123,451 acres: alpine and mountain forest.
    Exceptional Teton Mountains scenery.
    Near Driggs, Idaho.

North Absaroka Shoshone NF, 307-332-5460. Est. 1964.
    350,488 acres: alpine and mountain forest.
    Peaks up to 12,188 feet and is contiguous with the Absaroka-Beartooth
        east of Yellowstone.
    Near Cody.

Platte River Medicine Bow NF, 307-745-2300. Est. 1984.
    22,749 acres (743 in Colorado): river and grassland.
    Blue ribbon Platte River.
    Near Laramie.

Popo Agie Shoshone NF, 307-332-5460. Est. 1984.
    101,870 acres: alpine and mountain forest.
    Lakes, meadows, and peaks of the Wind River Range.
    Near Lander. $

Savage Run Medicine Bow NF, 307-745-2300. Est. 1978.
    14,930 acres: forest and canyons.
    The Savage Run Creek highlights this remote area.
    Near Laramie.

Teton Bridger-Teton NF, 307-739-5500. Est. 1964.
585,238 acres: alpine and mountain forest.
Headwaters of the Snake and Yellowstone W & SRs.
Near Jackson. 👟 ∪

Washakie Shoshone NF, 307-332-5460. Est. 1964.
704,822 acres: alpine and mountain forest.
Meadows and forests here are an essential part of the Greater
Yellowstone Ecosystem.
Near Dubois. 👟 ∪

Winegar Hole Targhee NF, 208-624-3151. Est. 1984.
10,715 acres: forest and meadows.
Habitat for grizzlies between Yellowstone and Grand Teton national
parks.
Near Flag Ranch. 👟

Areas Needing Your Support

Americans are very fortunate. No other country on earth shares with its citizens a real estate portfolio that compares to ours. This amazing collection of prime parcels includes the Grand Canyon, Yellowstone, Arctic National Wildlife Refuge, Everglades, and Yosemite, among many more natural treasures. Americans enjoy national forests, parks, and wildlife refuges too numerous to count. However, urban sprawl and commercial development creep into our wildlands, forests, marshes, and even nip at the deserts.

Unfortunately, legislation is being considered to gut environmental laws and open more wildlands to development. Congress is withholding Land and Water Conservation Fund monies intended to purchase threatened wilderness. Oil, gas, mining, and chemical companies continue to extract precious resources within and at the edge of national parks, monuments, and forests. The U.S. military is celebrating the end of the Cold War by expanding training and combat facilities across public lands in the West.

The list below identifies fifteen wild places that we consider the most endangered. To produce this list, we examined the natural significance of the area and the seriousness and immanence of the threat. While such judgments may be subjective, there is no doubt that the threat to each of these is significant, nor is there any doubt that these places are worth protecting. Our list includes:

Arctic National Wildlife Refuge, Alaska

Our nation's largest, and arguably wildest, wildlife refuge. The oil industry has been trying for years to obtain permission to drill here. The estimated amount of oil underneath the refuge offers no substantial evidence of an oil supply that would last more than a few months. More than 200 species depend on the refuge for survival, including moose, caribou, polar bears, grizzly bears, wolves, and others.

Badger–Two Medicine, Montana

Chevron USA and Fina Oil have sought to drill and develop oil and natural gas wells in the Badger–Two Medicine for more than a decade. Both companies hold leases to thousands of acres in this area. According to the USDA Forest Service, the chance of discovering oil or gas is less than 1 percent. The area is considered sacred to the neighboring Blackfeet tribe and essential habitat for grizzly bears.

Boundary Waters Canoe Area Wilderness, Minnesota

Although the Wilderness Act of 1964 banned roads and motorized recreation in wilderness areas, pre-existing conditions of float plane and snowmobile use in this area were allowed to continue after the wilderness's designation. A deal cut in Congress between two Minnesota representatives would allow increased motorized access to the Boundary Water Canoe Area.

Cabeza Prieta National Wildlife Refuge, Arizona

Home to many desert animals, including the endangered desert pronghorn, the future of the Cabeza Prieta and the adjacent Barry M. Goldwater Range is uncertain. The Marine Corps may use the area as a fly-by zone for loud jets and military helicopters.

Cascade Crest, Washington

Clear-cut logging of steep slopes and urban growth threaten many areas in the Cascades east of Seattle. Forty thousand acres of privately owned roadless land still exists in the Central Cascades, and it could cost more than $400 million to acquire and protect that acreage as wilderness.

Cumberland Island National Seashore, Georgia

Four private tracts of land in the middle of this established seashore are now up for sale—about 1,000 acres of potential habitat loss. With The Nature Conservancy, the owners are negotiating the sale of land to the park, but Congress must authorize the funds to finish the deal.

Izembek National Wildlife Refuge, Alaska

Congress is considering legislation to authorize construction of a road through 18 miles of the Izembek NWR, including 7 miles of its designated wilderness area. The road would connect the fishing village of King Cove to the community of Cold Bay, providing access to a large airport built during World War II. The road would have detrimental impact on the Peninsula Caribou Herd and many migratory birds.

Klamath Basin National Wildlife Refuges, Oregon

Essential wetland habitat has been severely degraded by tens of thousands of acres with chemically intensive commercial agriculture and their nonpoint source pollution. In addition, 15,000 acres of the Tule Lake National Wildlife Refuge and 11,000 acres of the Lower Klamath National Wildlife Refuge are used to cultivate potatoes, onions, sugar beets, and other crops.

Mojave Desert, California

Although much of the California desert is protected under the California Desert Protection Act, the U.S. Army wants to add another 331,000 acres to its already 3 million acres of training grounds for additional tank warfare training. This will continue the further encroachment on desert wildlife such as the desert tortoise, bighorn sheep, and others.

Okefenokee National Wildlife Refuge, Georgia and Florida

This vast forest wetland of peat-covered prairies, lakes, cypress forests, pine woods, and hardwood hammocks may be affected by a proposed mine nearby. E. I. Du Pont De Nemours and Company wants to develop a titanium mine on 38,000 acres of the Trail Ridge, which runs along the eastern boundary of Okefenokee.

Owyhee Canyonlands,
Idaho, Nevada, and Oregon

The Air Force and the BLM have reached an agreement on plans to create a bombing range in the Owyhee Canyonlands of Idaho, Nevada, and Oregon. Under the agreement, 12,000 acres of public land would be given to the military. The plan would allow flights as low as 1,000 feet over this area and threaten bighorn sheep populations.

Petroglyph National Monument, New Mexico

The plan is to build a six-lane freeway outside of Albuquerque, New Mexico, an area with more than 15,000 petroglyphs. Also, the building of an 18,000-home development nearby has been proposed.

Routt National Forest, Colorado

Damaging logging practices threaten many acres of habitat for elk, mountain lions, and other forest mammals.

Utah Wilderness, Utah

The amount of land proposed by the BLM for wilderness designation has historically been a far cry from what conservationists would consider acceptable. While bureaucrats try to determine what is and what is not worth preserving, precious wilderness is slipping away. The White River has been scarred by oil and gas development. Road construction and range projects have whittled down the North Stansburys Area in the West Desert. Even so, other industrial ventures continue to threaten Utah Wilderness.

Western Maine Woods, Maine

In June 1998, nearly 5 percent of the state of Maine was put up for sale by Sappi Fine Paper North America. The wild quality of these lands is legendary. The AT crosses the area in five different places. It contains many miles of habitat for moose, black bear, and other forest animals.

The Wilderness Society is committed to creating a nationwide wilderness network. The Wilderness Society's vision includes not only the vast landscapes such as the Grand Canyon, but also the small city parks and suburban meadows. This vision will never become reality unless we can first fend off the threats to our already preserved wilderness.

We have just begun to turn away from the notion of wilderness as a place to be tamed, as a resource to be extracted, as grasslands to be grazed. We now recognize its recreational value and the role wilderness plays in purifying our air and water. Our wildlands anchor local economies and serve as natural laboratories, holding microbes and plants that could unlock many of nature's mysteries.

As we approach the 50th anniversary (1999) of the publication of The Wilderness Society founder Aldo Leopold's classic, *A Sand County Almanac,* it is important that we reflect on the "land ethic" he set forth. His land ethic changes the role of humans from conquerors of the land-community to members and citizens of it; we are a part of a natural community that includes soils, water, plants, and animals. We must respect the community and all its members. "A thing is right," he said, "only when it tends to preserve the integrity, stability, and beauty of the community. It is wrong when it tends otherwise."

Index of Wilderness Areas